KNIGHTS OF CHRIST

LIVING TODAY WITH THE VIRTUES
OF ANCIENT KNIGHTHOOD

DANIEL A. BIDDLE

WESTBOW
PRESS
A DIVISION OF THOMAS NELSON

For web resources and teaching videos related to this book, see http://www.KnightsofChrist.com

WestBow Press books may be ordered through booksellers or by contacting:

WestBow Press
A Division of Thomas Nelson
1663 Liberty Drive
Bloomington, IN 47403
www.westbowpress.com
1-(866) 928-1240

ISBN: 978-1-4497-5043-5 (sc)
ISBN: 978-1-4497-5042-8 (hc)
ISBN: 978-1-4497-5044-2 (e)

Library of Congress Control Number: 2012907931

Printed in the United States of America

WestBow Press rev. date: 05/09/2012

To my wife, Jennifer, who supported me in this work

To Makaela, Alyssa, Matthew, and Amanda, and
to your children and your children's children for a
hundred generations—this book is for all of you

To my first knights: John (the Perceptive Knight), Maxwell
(the Well-Rounded Knight), Christian (the Determined
Knight), Benjamin (the Warrior Knight), Parker (the Knight
with Love for every soul), Parker (the Perseverant Knight
who never stops—yes, both of you!), and Justin and Bradley
(the Brother Knights who together can slay any dragon)

To the Duke, Pastor Mark Johnston, who
has trained an army of knights

And to Leigh Bashor and Jenny Arnez, whose
labor greatly refined this work

Thank you all

Hail be to Christ, the First Knight

> You are the most excellent of men and your lips have been anointed with grace, since God has blessed you forever. Gird your sword upon your side, O mighty one; clothe yourself with splendor and majesty. In your majesty ride forth victoriously in behalf of truth, humility and righteousness; let your right hand display awesome deeds. Let your sharp arrows pierce the hearts of the king's enemies; let the nations fall beneath your feet. Your throne, O God, will last forever and ever; a scepter of justice will be the scepter of your kingdom.
>
> —Psalm 45:2-6

> "I have found that most young people really want us to spell out a moral code. They may not accept it or believe it, but they want to hear it, clearly and without compromise."
>
> —Graham[1]

CONTENTS

PREFACE

Some who read this book may mistake it for simply a review of rules for religiously living the Christian faith. It is not. This book describes twenty-four virtues that will protect your life against frivolous and void living and fill it with power, meaning, and faith. They will even protect you against troubles—troubles that you can bring on yourself by not living according to the twenty-four virtues of knighthood.

View these virtues as the structure for your life—the backbone. These traits, like a knight's armor, will protect and guide you so you can find *and* keep the journey the Lord desires for your life (Jeremiah 29:11; 2 Chronicles 7:14). But these virtues must also be coupled with a life lived with passion, heart, love, and grace. Without these, the virtues of knighthood can be reduced to just rules, legalism, and a life lived as a "clanging gong" (1 Corinthians 13:1).

Living under the Order of Knighthood means that a person has determined to do just that—live *under* the Order defined by these twenty-four virtues. Knights live fully subjected to the virtues of the Order—to the point where they govern his behaviors on a daily basis, no matter what the circumstances. A knight is one who takes 1 Timothy 6:11 seriously: "But you, man of God, flee from all this, and pursue righteousness, godliness, faith, love, endurance, and gentleness."

By living according to these virtues, a person can obtain the *confidence* of the living God and be put into a position where he is regularly used by God for His purposes: "For the Lord detests a perverse man but *takes the upright into his confidence*" (Proverbs 3:32, emphasis added). Scripture gives direct promises to enlist us in God's personal service if we do so.

If a man cleanses himself from the latter [wickedness and godless living], he will be an instrument for noble purposes, made holy, useful to the Master and prepared to do any good work (2 Timothy 2:21).

The Lord confides in those who fear him; he makes his covenant known to them (Psalm 25:14).

Living a life subjected to the Holy Spirit will naturally produce these traits in one's life: "And God is able to make all grace abound to you, so that in all things at all times, having all that you need, you will abound in every good work" (2 Corinthians 9:8). Jesus is the author and finisher of our lives and yearns to live through us in powerful ways (Philippians 1:6).

Before diving into this book on biblical and knightly virtues, let's review just one more thing: Just what is *Christian virtue*? A set of Sunday school rules? Rules for living like a good Christian? Actually, they are neither. They are slightly more complicated.

Put simply, Christian virtues are the "thou *shalls*" of Christianity—they represent what you *should* be doing with your life and how you should be living as God intended to both enjoy your life and make the impact you were intended to make while on this earth.

Virtue also differs from rule-keeping because it has to do with character. Character is much more than rule-keeping—it is about who you are as a person, what you stand for, how you respond to tough situations, what you are willing to compromise for, and what you will not. N. T. Wright puts it this way: "Jesus Himself, backed up by the early Christian writers, speaks repeatedly about the development of a particular *character*. Character—the transforming, shaping, and marking of a life and its habits—will generate the sort of behavior that rules might have pointed toward but which a 'rule-keeping' *mentality* can never achieve. And it will produce the sort of life which will in fact be true to itself . . ." (emphases added)[2]

And virtue, when practiced continually, builds a life of character. Action by action, choice by choice, virtue transforms you into a person of true character: "Virtue, in this strict sense, is what happens when someone has made a thousand small choices, requiring effort and concentration, to do something which is good and right but which doesn't 'come naturally'—and then, on a thousand and first time, when it really matters, they find that they do what's required 'automatically.'"[3]

Finally, virtuous living should not be viewed as the opposite of living freely and gracefully by the Holy Spirit and having a life marked by the *fruit* of the Spirit (Galatians 5:22-23). As Wright also points out, "Christian virtue, including the nine-fold fruit of the Spirit is *both* the gift of God *and* the result of the person of faith making conscious decisions to cultivate this way of life and these habits of heart and mind."[4] Wright continues to make the point that if we are going to grow fruit of the Spirit, we need to *tend the tree that produces it.*

All who strive to live by these virtues will experience challenge and struggle in this life—but they will also experience lasting blessings and a life full of meaning and richness in the eyes of God. In Christ, we are given both the freedom to strive to live by these virtues and the grace to try again when we fall. "Though a righteous man falls seven times, he rises again, but the wicked are brought down by calamity" (Proverbs 24:16). May your journey be filled with grace, purpose, power, and love.

REFLECT

> I no longer call you servants, because a servant does not know his master's business. Instead, I have called you friends, for everything that I learned from my Father I have made known to you. You did not choose me, but I chose you and appointed you to go and bear fruit—fruit that will last. Then the Father will give you whatever you ask in my name. This is my command: Love each other.
>
> —John 15:15-17

All God's revelations are sealed until they are opened to us by obedience. You will never get them open by philosophy or thinking. Immediately you obey, a flash of light comes. Let God's truth work in you by soaking in it, not by worrying into it. The only way you can get to know is to stop trying to find out and by being born again. Obey God in the thing He shows you, and instantly the next thing is opened up. One reads tomes on the work of the Holy Spirit, when one five minutes of drastic obedience would make things as clear as a sunbeam. "I suppose I shall understand these things some day!" You can understand them now. It is not study that does it, but obedience. The tiniest fragment of obedience, and heaven opens and the profoundest truths of God are yours straight away. God will never reveal more truth about Himself until you have obeyed what you know already. Beware of becoming wise and prudent.[5]

—Oswald Chambers

For web resources and teaching videos related to this book, see http://www.KnightsofChrist.com

INTRODUCTION

Have you ever found yourself sitting with friends after watching a great medieval knight movie and your friends are saying, "That was a cool movie," while you are thinking, "No—that was a *really cool* movie" and finding yourself reflecting on some of the deeper meanings in the movie? If this is true about you, the chances are you will enjoy this book.

History tells us that real knights lived, and that they were different. They were different because many of them took their Christianity, their code of ethics, and their life ethos very seriously. As the movie about the Navy SEALs, *Act of Valor*, opens, the narrator reads a letter explaining that every man must have a code, an ethos, a set of convictions that dictate his purpose and behavior in life. This code "forms the box" in which he lives and moves and makes decisions. This book provides such an ethos for today's Christian. No, I am not talking about legalism or keeping some regimented list of rules or regulations. I am talking about character, conviction, and true Christianity. I am talking about a life modeled after the psalmist who wrote: "My soul *followeth hard* after thee: thy right hand upholdeth me" (Psalm 63:8, KJV, emphasis added).

Why is this important? Because the statement "Those who do not stand for something will fall for anything" is true. If you are not quite sure you believe this, just take a look around in your life. How are your friends turning out? Are the majority of your childhood friends currently living God-honoring lives? Are they living *with* God, *through* God, and *for* God on a daily basis?

That is where this book can make a difference. By learning these twenty-four knightly virtues and why the medieval knights chose to live by them, you can strengthen your personal ethos and develop one that is based firmly on God's "DNA for life" contained in Scripture.

What is the result of living such a life? God's promises for those who live their lives to honor Him are incredible. Here is just a sample of the promises that are issued to you personally from the God of the Universe:

> For the eyes of the Lord range throughout the earth to strengthen those whose hearts are fully committed to him (2 Chronicles 16:9).

> A faithful man will be richly blessed, but one eager to get rich will not go unpunished (Proverbs 28:20).

> Blessed is the man who finds wisdom, the man who gains understanding, for she is more profitable than silver and yields better returns than gold. She is more precious than rubies; nothing you desire can compare with her. Long life is in her right hand; in her left hand are riches and honor. Her ways are pleasant ways, and all her paths are peace. She is a tree of life to those who embrace her; those who lay hold of her will be blessed (Proverbs 3:13-18).

When the Bible makes promises like these, they can be counted on. The Old Testament (particularly Psalms and Proverbs—e.g., Proverbs 10-11) are filled with contrasting promises—promises that assure that those who order their lives after God's ways and those who choose to carve out their own way of living will have very different lives—both now and for eternity.

While we have our eternal destiny secure if we have truly trusted in Christ for our salvation, we will experience more than our share of struggle in this life if we live against God's ways:

If they have escaped the corruption of the world by knowing our Lord and Savior Jesus Christ and are again entangled in it and overcome, they are worse off at the end than they were at the beginning. It would have been better for them not to have known the way of righteousness than to have known it and then to turn their backs on the sacred command that was passed on to them. Of them the proverbs are true: "A dog returns to its vomit," and, "A sow that is washed goes back to her wallowing in the mud" (2 Peter 2:20-22).

So how do we avoid this struggle—one where we continually cycle our lives back into the web of sin that is so effective at destroying our lives and stealing God's best for us? By living under the grace and guidance of the Holy Spirit and by following God's Word in a way that it becomes a daily habit and part of our deep-seated character. This book will help you do both of these.

This does not imply that God runs around sprinkling daily blessings into the lives of his "good children" and cursing the lives of the wicked. Rather, challenges come into the lives of those who pursue God and those who have forsaken Him. But we get to choose how we respond and which road we will take along our journey of life:

Wisdom calls aloud in the street, she raises her voice in the public squares; at the head of the noisy streets she cries out, in the gateways of the city she makes her speech: "How long will you simple ones love your simple ways? How long will mockers delight in mockery and fools hate knowledge? If you had responded to my rebuke, I would have poured out my heart to you and made my thoughts known to you. But since you rejected me when I called and no one gave heed when I stretched out my hand, since you ignored all my advice and would not accept my rebuke, I in turn will laugh at your disaster; I will mock when calamity overtakes you—when calamity overtakes you like a storm, when disaster sweeps over you like a whirlwind, when distress and trouble overwhelm you. Then they will call to me but I will not answer; they will look for me but will not find me. Since they hated knowledge and did not choose to fear the Lord, since they would not accept my advice and spurned my rebuke, they will eat the fruit of their ways and be filled with the fruit of their schemes. For the waywardness of the simple will kill them, and the complacency of fools will destroy them; but whoever listens to me will live in safety and be at ease, without fear of harm (Proverbs 1:20-33).

This passage presents the truth that we all have choices to make—choices to take God's way or our way at several life junctures that we face every day. This passage is not asserting, and neither is the author, that those who follow God's way will live happy, unblemished, and unchallenged lives. Rather, challenges flow into everyone's lives, but this book will help guide your choices to minimize the extra challenges we sometimes create for ourselves by making choices that stray from God's path.

But wait a minute . . . Christians are under grace and not the law, i.e., moral codes and practices, correct? Yes, we are under grace. Christ's sacrifice has removed the consequences from the law from our lives: "Before this faith came, we were held prisoners by the law, locked up until faith should be revealed. So the law was put in charge to lead us to Christ that we might be justified by faith. Now that faith has come, we are no longer under the supervision of the law" (Galatians 3:23-25).

But being under grace and not the law does not mean that we abandon purity and upright living. To the contrary, under grace, we live to obey Christ and pursue righteousness out of our love for Him rather than using our "grace card" as a license to sin ("For certain men whose condemnation was written about long ago have secretly slipped in among you. They are godless men, who change the grace of our God into a license for immorality and deny Jesus Christ our only Sovereign and Lord" (Jude 1:4). In fact, the Bible says that true salvation will lead to a changed life—one marked by upright living and good deeds:

> What good is it, my brothers, if a man claims to have faith but has no deeds? Can such faith save him? Suppose a brother or sister is without clothes and daily food. If one of you says to him, "Go, I wish you well; keep warm and well fed," but does nothing about his physical needs, what good is it? In the same way, faith by itself, if it is not accompanied by action, is dead. But someone will say, "You have faith; I have deeds." Show me your faith without deeds, and I will show you my faith by what I do. You believe that there is one God. Good! Even the demons believe that—and shudder. You foolish man, do you want evidence that faith without deeds is useless? Was not our ancestor Abraham considered righteous for what he did when he offered his son Isaac on the altar? You see that his faith and his actions were working together, and his faith was made complete by what he did. And the scripture was fulfilled that says, "Abraham believed God, and it was credited to him as righteousness," and he was called God's friend. You see that a person is justified by what he does and not by faith alone. In the same way, was not even Rahab the prostitute considered righteous for what she did when she gave lodging to the spies and sent them off in a different

direction? As the body without the spirit is dead, so faith without deeds is dead (James 2:18-25).

Finally, Christ says that one of the most visible and assuring marks of a true Christian is whether we obey His commands:

> If you love me, you will obey what I command (John 14:15).

> Whoever has my commands and obeys them, he is the one who loves me. He who loves me will be loved by my Father, and I too will love him and show myself to him (John 14:21).

> If anyone loves me, he will obey my teaching. My Father will love him, and we will come to him and make our home with him. He who does not love me will not obey my teaching. These words you hear are not my own; they belong to the Father who sent me (John 14:23-24).

> If you obey my commands, you will remain in my love, just as I have obeyed my Father's commands and remain in his love. I have told you this so that my joy may be in you and that your joy may be complete. My command is this: Love each other as I have loved you. Greater love has no one than this, that he lay down his life for his friends. You are my friends if you do what I command (John 15:10-14).

> Therefore go and make disciples of all nations, baptizing them in the name of the Father and of the Son and of the Holy Spirit, and teaching them to obey everything I have commanded you. And

surely I am with you always, to the very end of the age (Matthew 28:19-20).

As Jesus was saying these things, a woman in the crowd called out, "Blessed is the mother who gave you birth and nursed you." He replied, "Blessed rather are those who hear the word of God and obey it" (Luke 11:27-28).

Therefore everyone who hears these words of mine and puts them into practice is like a wise man who built his house on the rock. The rain came down, the streams rose, and the winds blew and beat against that house; yet it did not fall, because it had its foundation on the rock. But everyone who hears these words of mine and does not put them into practice is like a foolish man who built his house on sand. The rain came down, the streams rose, and the winds blew and beat against that house, and it fell with a great crash (Matthew 7:24-27).

The apostles echo these same teachings:

Everyone who believes that Jesus the Christ is born of God, and everyone who loves the father loves his child as well. This is how we know that we love the children of God: by loving God and carrying out his commands. This is love for God: to obey his commands. And his commands are not burdensome, for everyone born of God overcomes the world. This is the victory that has overcome the world, even our faith (1 John 5:1-4).

And now, dear lady, I am not writing you a new command but one we have had from the beginning.

I ask that we love one another. And this is love: that we walk in obedience to his commands. As you have heard from the beginning, his command is that you walk in love (2 John 1:5-6).

Therefore, my dear friends, as you have always obeyed—not only in my presence, but now much more in my absence—continue to work out your salvation with fear and trembling (Philippians 2:12).

Finally, one dynamic that occurs with Christians who strive on the narrow way is the promised filling and empowering of the Holy Spirit. While we receive the Holy Spirit when we receive Christ, the continual filling of the Holy Spirit partly depends on our chosen lifestyle (i.e., to obey Christ versus living constantly in sin):

We are witnesses of these things, and so is the Holy Spirit, whom God has given *to those who obey him* (Acts 5:32, emphasis added).

And do not grieve the Holy Spirit of God, with whom you were sealed for the day of redemption (Ephesians 4:30).

Yet they rebelled and grieved his Holy Spirit. So he turned and became their enemy and he himself fought against them (Isaiah 63:10).

Do not put out the Spirit's fire (1 Thessalonians 5:19).

Do you want a life filled with power from the Holy Spirit? Daily insight on which choices to make along life's complex path? Reassurance that you are heading in the best direction in life? The Holy Spirit provides all of this, and we keep His presence in our lives when we walk straight and our lifestyles honor the One who gave us freedom from the law and the command to become slaves to righteousness instead:

> Don't you know that when you offer yourselves to someone to obey him as slaves, you are slaves to the one whom you obey—whether you are slaves to sin, which leads to death, or to obedience, which leads to righteousness? But thanks be to God that, though you used to be slaves to sin, you wholeheartedly obeyed the form of teaching to which you were entrusted. You have been set free from sin and have become slaves to righteousness (Romans 6:16-18).

Living this way moves us to God's fast track to be used for our ultimate purpose on Earth: "If a man cleanses himself from the latter, he will be an instrument for noble purposes, made holy, useful to the Master and prepared to do any good work" (2 Timothy 2:21).

The Calling of Knighthood

Knights who lived during the peak of the medieval era believed that the office of knighthood was nothing short of a Divine calling where God Himself chose a knight among one thousand men and appointed him to live in the Order of Knighthood. Such individuals— those who believed they were called to be knights—volunteered (or were raised) in the Order of Knighthood and were appointed into the Order by other knights, barons, or church officials.

But what about today? Does this Divine Order of Knighthood still exist? I believe it does—not by some appointing authority like the church or a queen, but by a person's life choices made on a day-by-day basis. For even if a person could achieve a formal dubbing by some worldly authority (as was U2's lead singer, Bono, when he was dubbed a knight by the Queen of England), only a person's lifestyle choices can attest to whether he will live up to the title of "Knight."

To begin your journey of knighthood, let's first take a look into the ancient origins of knighthood. The Book of the Order of Chivalry (Knighthood) was written about 1275 by Ramon Lull, an ancient writer and philosopher of the thirteenth century. This book is now regarded as one of the most insightful works into what knighthood was like in medieval times. It was originally written in Catalan and then translated into French and finally English in the fifteenth century. One of the English translations was completed in 1484 by William Caxton. This version is said to best preserve the meaning of the original work by Lull.

The introduction of this book is incredible and is provided in its entirety below.[6] The story begins by telling the tale of a seasoned knight who has become a hermit, retiring after decades of battle and tournaments. As this hermit rests one quiet morning in prayer in a meadow near a fountain, a young squire (an aspiring knight candidate), who has fallen asleep on his horse, strays into the meadow and wakes up when the horse drinks from the fountain. Catching sight of the hermit, he dismounts. Each is surprised at the other's presence. The story continues . . .

> The Hermit knew that the Squire would not speak first out of reverence, so he spoke first and said, "Fair friend, what is your desire or intent on where you are going; and why have you come here?" "Sire," he said, "It is widespread news that a wise and noble king has commanded a great Feast and will himself be made a new knight and afterwards will dub and make other new knights, of both foreign and local men. And I am therefore going to this Feast to be dubbed a knight. But when I was asleep because of

the hardship of my great journeys that I have made, my horse went out of the right way and brought me to this place."

When the Hermit heard him speak of knighthood, and he remembered the Order of Knighthood that pertains to a knight, he cast out a great sigh and entered in great thought, remembering the honor in which knighthood had been long maintained. While the Hermit was in deep thought, the Squire demanded to know what was so burdening his heart.

And the Hermit answered him, "Fair son, my thought is of the Order of Knighthood and of the greatness in which a knight is held in maintaining the greatness of the honor of knighthood." Then the Squire pleaded to the Hermit to tell him about the order and the manner of knighthood, and how he could live as a true knight in the way that would be most honoring to God.

"How, son," said the Hermit, "how do you know what is the rule and order of knighthood? And I marvel how you dare demand knighthood before you know the Order. For no knight may love the Order, or even what pertains to this Order, unless he can know the faults that he does against the Order of Knighthood. Indeed, no knight ought to make any knights unless he himself knows the Order of Knighthood. For a knight who does not live as a knight cannot show others the order or the custom of Knighthood."

While the Hermit said these words to the Squire—
words that explained that a knight should first
know the things of knighthood before he should
seek becoming a knight—the Squire answered and
said to the Hermit, "Sir, if it be your pleasure, I
plead with you to tell me about the true Order of
Knighthood. For I now believe that I should learn
what it truly means to be a knight before seeking to
become one. And, if you allow, I will seek to become
a knight with all of my power if you would please
teach me and show me how to become a knight.

"Friend," said the Hermit, "the rule and Order of
Knighthood is written in this little book that I hold
here in my hands, which I study and which makes
me remember and think on the grace and bounty
that God has given and done to me in this world
because I honored and maintained the Order of
Knighthood with all my power. For as knighthood
gives to a knight all that belongs to him, a knight
ought to give all his forces to honor knighthood."

Then the Hermit delivered to the Squire the little
book. And when he had read therein, he understood
that the knight only among a thousand persons is
chosen worthy to have more noble office than all
the thousand. And he had also understood by that
little book the rule and order of knighthood. And
then he paused in reflection for a short time and
said, "Ah Sir, blessed are you that have brought me
in this place and in time that I have knowledge of
knighthood, which I have long desired without that
I knew the nobleness of the order nor the honor in
which our Lord God has set all them that be in the
Order of Knighthood."

The Hermit said, "Fair son, I am an old man and feeble and may not therefore live much longer. And therefore this little book that is made for the devotion, loyalty, and the ordinance that a knight ought to have in holding his order, you shall bring with you to the Feast where you can go and show it to all of them who would desire to become knights. And when you shall be a newly dubbed knight and return into your country, come again to this place and let me have knowledge of those who have become new knights and shall be obedient to the doctrine of knighthood." Then the Hermit gave to the Squire his blessing, and he left him and took the book with him in devotion. And he mounted his horse and left hastily for the Feast. And when he arrived at the Feast, he presented the book wisely to the noble king, and offered that every noble man that would be in the Order of Knighthood might have a copy of the little book to the end that he might see and learn the Order of Knighthood.

No one will ever really know if this was an actual encounter between the Hermit Knight and the Squire. Nonetheless, the information contained in the "little book" (written over five hundred years ago) lives on today, and much of it has been included in this work. The second chapter of the "little book" describes the beginning of the Order of Knighthood:

When charity, royalty, truth, justice, and verity fail in the world, then began cruelty, injury, disloyalty, and falseness. And therefore error and trouble entered into the world in which God had created man in intention that of the man he be known and loved, feared, served, and honored. At the beginning, when crime came into the world, justice returned through fear to the honor in which justice needs to be. And therefore all the people were divided into thousands. And of each thousand was chosen a man most loyal, most strong, and of most noble courage and better taught and mannered than all the others. He was inquired and searched for, he who was best and was convenably most fair, most courageous, and most able to sustain trials, and the most able to serve mankind.

A true knight is a person whose lifestyle and virtues set him or her apart as "one in a thousand." This is even echoed in Ecclesiastes 7:27-28: "'Look,' says the Teacher, 'This is what I have discovered: Adding one thing to another to discover the scheme of things—while I was still searching but not finding—I found one upright man among a thousand.'"

There are no half knights. Living under the Order of Knighthood means that a person has determined to do just that—live *under* the Order. While this book contains twenty-four virtues of knighthood, one can find similar books (both modern and old) that contain other sets of virtues that almost always overlap. Whatever the set of virtues, a true knight lives fully subjected to them so they govern his behaviors on a daily basis, no matter what the circumstances.

WOMEN KNIGHTS

Knights are typically thought of as only men. History (and sainthood, as shown by the life of Joan of Arc), however, shows that the office of knighthood was also open to whatever woman wanted to live like one. Joan of Arc was arguably one of the bravest and most dedicated knights to ever live, both men and women included. Even while being burned at the stake, she stayed faithful to her faith and calling. She foretold her own injury on the day she was shot with an arrow but went into battle regardless. When it happened, she was brought back to safety and pulled out the arrow herself, which was driven all the way through her shoulder and out her back. Hours later, she returned to battle and led her troops to victory.

Joan was also passionate about purity. She regularly scorned those who used foul language in her presence. When it came to sexual purity, she was uncompromising. When she led her knights triumphantly into town after battle, the local prostitutes would flock her knights with solicitations. History records that in some situations she dealt with them with firm grace; in other situations, however, she dealt with them harshly:

> Indeed, once near the town of Chateau-Thierry, when she saw the mistress of one of the soldiers, who was a knight, she chased her with a naked sword. But she did not strike the woman. She warned her gently and kindly that she must never appear in soldiers' company again, or she, Joan, would do something to her that she would dislike. D'Alencon's account was more violent: "Joan was chaste, and she loathed those women who follow the soldiers. I once saw her at Saint Denis, on the way back from the king's coronation, chase a girl who was with the soldiers so hard that she broke her sword."[7]

Joan was a poor peasant girl born in France who claimed to hear divine voices from angels and God himself—voices that led her to lead the French armies to victory over the English in many occasions during the Hundred Years War between the two countries. After leading the French army for just over one year, she was captured, sold to the English, tried by the Catholic Church, and burned at the stake as a heretic. Twenty-five years after her execution, the pope retried her case and pronounced her innocent, changing her position from witch to martyr. Hundreds of years later (in 1920), she was canonized as a saint. Below are some examples of female knights and knightly orders:

- In 1762, a famous chemist and historian named Elias Ashmole wrote about women becoming knights in his book titled the *Institution, Laws, and Ceremony of the Most Noble Order of the Garter*.[8]
- Nobleman Loderigo d'Andalo of Bologna founded the Knightly Order of the Glorious Saint Mary in 1233. This order was formally approved by the Pope in 1261 and granted military status to women.
- In modern days, some French orders include women. For example, the Légion d'Honneur (Legion of Honor) has admitted female knights since the mid-1900s (called *chevaliers*). The first documented case is that of Marie-Angélique Duchemin (1772-1859), who fought in the Revolutionary Wars and received a military disability pension in 1798, the rank of second lieutenant in 1822, and the Legion of Honor in 1852.
- Between 1358 and 1488, sixty-eight women were inducted into the Order of the Garter.
- Queen Mary was the first European woman to be granted knighthood and was made a Knight Grand Commander of the same order in 1911. She was also granted a knighthood in 1917 when the Order of the British Empire was created, an order that was the first to be explicitly open to women.
- The Royal Victorian Order was opened to women in 1936 and the Orders of Bath and Saint Michael and Saint George in 1965 and 1971, respectively. Queen consorts have been made Ladies of the Garter since 1901 (Queens Alexandra in 1901, Mary in 1910, and Elizabeth in 1937).

A True Knight Serves All but Loves Only One

The first lesson in knighthood is that a true knight serves only the king. His allegiance cannot be divided among others, including himself. This means a knight must *live for an audience of One.*[9] We should focus on living for God and pleasing Him as our only audience. We should not fear our enemies or any other mortal person more than God. Scripture makes clear that our devotion to Christ the King should be undeniably first in our lives:

> When God rescued Daniel from the fiery furnace, even the worldly king acknowledged this truth: "Then Nebuchadnezzar said, 'Praise be to the God of Shadrach, Meshach, and Abednego who has sent his angel and rescued his servants! They trusted in him and defied the king's command and were willing to give up their lives rather than serve or worship any god except their own God'" (Daniel 3:28).

> I have been crucified with Christ and I no longer live, but Christ lives in me. The life I live in the body, I live by faith in the Son of God, who loved me and gave himself for me (Galatians 2:20).

> Servants, be subject to them which are your masters according to the flesh with fear and trembling, in singleness of your heart as unto Christ (Ephesians 6:5).

I once heard a sermon where the pastor said, "Every time we sin, we have a belief problem." He explained that if we really, honestly, completely believed that Christ was in the invisible spiritual space next to us, we would be less inclined to sin. Living for God alone is difficult, especially when we cannot see God yet can see people.

But Christ encourages us: "Do not be afraid of those who kill the body but cannot kill the soul. Rather, be afraid of the one who can destroy both soul and body in hell" (Matthew 10:28). We should fear God, not man: "Fear of man will prove to be a snare, but whoever trusts in the Lord is kept safe" (Proverbs 29:25). The disciple Peter demonstrated this deep-seated confidence when he was brought before the Sanhedrin for questioning. The high priest's first accusation was, "We gave you strict orders not to teach in this name, yet you have filled Jerusalem with your teaching . . ." To this, Peter replied, "We must obey God rather than men!" (Acts 5:27-29).

Fear of man is a problem, especially when God is small and people are big. Fearing God means to have reverence and an attitude of deep respect for God. May the Lord encourage you to live with this long-term perspective, for the journey does not end when we are finished on Earth but continues much, much beyond.

THE TWENTY-FOUR VIRTUES
OF A TRUE KNIGHT

Lists of knightly virtues typically range from five to twelve[10] and typically include at least the "core" seven that were originally framed (in the context of knighthood) by Ramon Lull. While these seven virtues have their earlier origin in Catholic tradition and doctrine, Ramon Lull framed them in the context of knighthood in the thirteenth century as:

> First and foremost, if a knight not be of good *faith*, all is for naught that he does, for he may never have the other virtues or good customs, but for faith all is but sin that every man does. With Faith, men have hope, charity, and are servants to truth.

> *Hope* is a noble virtue, which causes knights to trust to have victory in battle. With hope, he has more trust in God, not in his horse, harness, or sword. Through hope, the courage of knights is reinforced, and cowardice overthrown. Hope is the principal instrument that governs knighthood in honor.

> A knight that does not have *charity* will be cruel and evil, which does not agree with the honor of knighthood.

All knights are needful of *justice*, for a knight without justice is without honor, and without justice there can be no knighthood. An injurious knight is an enemy of justice, and casts himself out of the order.

Prudence is a virtue that knights must have. It is a knowledge that men have of good and evil, and though which they become the enemy of evil and friend to all good things.

The virtue of *temperance* is the knowledge of the middle way between too much and too little, and the knowledge of one's own measure. The knight who is temperate in largess (being generous with gifts) gives neither too much nor too little; he is neither a coward nor foolhardy; in eating and drinking he is neither a glutton nor so hungry that he is wretched; in speech he does not use too many words nor so few that he is not understood; also, in his clothing he is neither excessive or wretched. Temperance is the rule of all wisdom.

With *fortitude* [strength], the knight fights against his enemies though noblesse of heart, temperance, and abstinence. It makes him courageous and hardy.[11]

Another Code of Knighthood was written about by Roland, an eighth century knight whose honorable act of sacrifice saved Emperor Charlemagne's entire army (see his story in Virtue 13: Sacrifice). A famous song written about Roland in the eleventh century ("The Song of Roland") reveals that Charlemagne's Code of Chivalry (Knighthood) likely had seventeen traits:

1. To fear God and maintain His church.
2. To serve his leader in valor and faith.

3. To protect the weak and defenseless.
4. To give help or assistance to widows and orphans, especially in times of difficulty.
5. To refrain from making deliberate offenses against others.
6. To live by honor and for glory.
7. To despise monetary rewards (in other words, money should not be a knight's motive for virtuous action).
8. To fight for the welfare of all.
9. To obey those placed in authority.
10. To guard the honor of fellow knights.
11. To despise and shun unfairness, meanness, and deceit.
12. To keep faith.
13. At all times to speak the truth.
14. To persevere to the end in any enterprise begun.
15. To respect the honor of women.
16. Never to refuse a challenge from an equal.
17. Never to turn the back upon a foe.

The twenty-four virtues included in this book are closely aligned with the historic lists of five, seven, twelve, or seventeen knightly virtues. The first seven are taken directly from the historical list of the "core seven" that was most widely taught in medieval times (preceded only by godliness). These are followed by sixteen other virtues derived from the other historic lists or directly from Scripture. Some of the original virtues were split into two or more similar virtues, or new virtues were added that are parts of larger virtues. For example, the virtues of Sacrifice and Compassion are included in this book because they are virtues under the more-encompassing virtue of Love (or Charity) that was originally framed by Lull.

For each of the virtues described in the next section, one or more key Bible verses are used to anchor them in Scripture. While each virtue is grounded widely in Scripture, only a few key verses are used to represent each. Each set of verses is followed by a description of the virtue and historic and/or current examples of how the virtue manifests in modern life.

GODLINESS

Be imitators of God, therefore, as dearly loved children and live a life of love, just as Christ loved us and gave himself up for us as a fragrant offering and sacrifice to God.

—Ephesians 5:1-2

Being godly means imitating God in your daily life. Put simply, a godly person is one who responds to daily life activities and circumstances in the way that Christ would. Essentially, this means aspiring to godly virtues (such as those defined in this book) while avoiding sin. First Timothy 6:11 encourages us to "Flee from all this (sin), and pursue righteousness, godliness, faith, love, endurance, and gentleness." These two actions—fleeing sin and pursuing righteousness—are the two "action commands" of godliness that can be used guide your decisions in daily life situations.

But wait a minute . . . knights were warriors—how can a person be a warrior and godly at the same time? Even a quick tour through the Gospels shows that Christ had many warrior-like traits (although not in a violent sense). Christ stood up to wrongdoing and wrong-doers (John 8:1-11). He used physical force when appropriate (Mark 11:15-19) yet opposed violence (Matthew 18:11).

Even God Himself is often characterized as a strong, kind, gentle, all-powerful warrior:

> Out of the brightness of his presence clouds advanced, with hailstones and bolts of lightning. The Lord thundered from heaven; the voice of the Most High resounded. He shot his arrows and scattered the enemies, great bolts of lightning and routed them. The valleys of the sea were exposed and the foundations of the earth laid bare at your rebuke, O Lord, at the blast of breath from your nostrils (Psalm 18:12-15).

So there we have it—the very creator of life, God Himself, is displayed in Scripture as a warrior slinging hailstones, bolts of lightning, and arrows and capable of laying out the foundations of the earth by a massive blast from his nostrils.

In Isaiah 42:13 God "marches out like a mighty man, like a warrior he will stir up his zeal; with a shout he will raise the battle cry and will triumph over his enemies." In Exodus 15:3, the Lord "is a warrior, the Lord is his name." There should not be any doubt that God is—and was—the mightiest warrior of all time.

A famous medieval writer, Cistercian Abbot Bernard of Clairvaux, wrote a treatise to help inspire the (relatively new) Knights Templar Order in the early twelfth century. In describing the "ideal Christian knight," he wrote:

> These are Godly men who shun every excess in clothing and food. They live as brothers in joyful and sober company (with) one heart and one soul . . . There is no distinction of persons among them and deference is shown to merit rather than to noble blood. They rival one another in mutual consideration, and they carry one another's burdens, thus fulfilling the law of Christ.[12]

Bernard further described the virtues of this true Christian knight as, "humility, austerity, justice, obedience, unselfishness, and a single-minded zeal for Jesus Christ in defending the poor, the weak, the Church and persecuted Christians."

REFLECT

But among you there must not be even a hint of sexual immorality, or of any kind of impurity, or of greed, because these are improper for God's holy people. Nor should there be obscenity, foolish talk, or coarse joking, which are out of place, but rather thanksgiving. For of this you can be sure: No immoral, impure or greedy person—such a man is an idolater—has any inheritance in the kingdom of Christ and of God.

—Ephesians 5:3-5

Avoid every kind of evil. May God himself, the God of peace, sanctify you through and through. May your whole spirit, soul, and body be kept blameless at the coming of our Lord Jesus Christ. The one who calls you is faithful and he will do it.

—1 Thessalonians 5:22-24

RESPOND

1. How do the passages above encourage you to live a godly life?
2. What is godliness?
3. Where does it come from?
4. How do we maintain godliness, even when we sin and make mistakes?

5. What does a godly life look like?
6. What happens if we are not godly?
7. Can you think of a person (dead or alive) who is godly? How did they live that made their life godly? How did they recover from the mistakes in their lives?

VIRTUE 2

FAITH

And without faith it is impossible to please God, because anyone who comes to him must believe that he exists and that he rewards those who earnestly seek him.

—Hebrews 11:6

For I know the plans I have for you, declares the Lord, plans to prosper you and not to harm you, plans to give you hope and a future. Then you will call upon me and come and pray to me, and I will listen to you. You will seek me and find me when you seek me with all your heart. I will be found by you, declares the Lord.

—Jeremiah 29:11-14

F aith is when you trust God and His purpose in your circumstances more than the resources that appear to be available to fit them *as you understand them*. As Hebrews 11:1 states, "Now faith is being sure of what we hope for and certain of what we do not see."

Faith is critical to the knight, so I encourage the reader to slow down and take some time to fully digest this section. Faith is so critical to God that He has gone so far to tell that it is *impossible* to even please Him without faith: "And without faith it is impossible to please God, because anyone who comes to him must believe that he exists and that he rewards those who earnestly seek him" (Hebrews 11:6). And remember, a true knight's first mission and calling is to *please the King*.

Before taking a biblical and historical look into how knights of old applied their faith, let's first take a look at how faith can be practically applied in your life. Zechariah 4:6 states, "This is the word of the Lord to Zerubbabel: 'Not by might nor by power, but by my Spirit,' says the Lord Almighty." This verse shows that faith is what we rely on to get through difficult times in our lives. Faith—our belief in Christ and in His power—is how to pull through challenging times in our lives. Not by our ingenuity, strength, own power, or anything else within us.

Zerubbabel was the civic leader of Jerusalem who was charged with the responsibility of finishing the work of rebuilding the temple. The work had already started but then was met with opposition and stalled. Zerubbabel needed encouragement to carry on the work. This simple (single) verse in the Bible explains just how Zerubbabel was to accomplish the work and the process given to him by God: he was to do so *by the Spirit of God*. The word that was given to him from the Lord was not "buck up" or "saddle up"—it was "rely on the Lord."

The term *might* means a collective strength (e.g., the strength of an army). The term *power* deals with an individual's strength. So God was saying to Zerubbabel: "Not by the resources of many or one, but by My Spirit. It will not be by your cleverness, your ability, or your physical strength that the temple will be rebuilt, but by the Spirit of God."[13] Consider these Scripture passages that encourage our reliance on God alone, and not our own might, power, or ingenuity:

> Such confidence as this is ours through Christ before God. Not that we are competent in ourselves to claim anything for ourselves, but our competence comes from God. He has made us competent as ministers of a new covenant—not of the letter but

of the Spirit; for the letter kills, but the Spirit gives life (2 Corinthians 3:4-6).

I rejoice greatly in the Lord that at last you have renewed your concern for me. Indeed, you have been concerned, but you had no opportunity to show it. I am not saying this because I am in need, for I have learned to be content whatever the circumstances. I know what it is to be in need, and I know what it is to have plenty. I have learned the secret of being content in any and every situation, whether well fed or hungry, whether living in plenty or in want. I can do everything through him who gives me strength (Philippians 4:10-13).

Remain in me, and I will remain in you. No branch can bear fruit by itself; it must remain in the vine. Neither can you bear fruit unless you remain in me. I am the vine; you are the branches. If a man remains in me and I in him, he will bear much fruit; apart from me you can do nothing. If anyone does not remain in me, he is like a branch that is thrown away and withers; such branches are picked up, thrown into the fire and burned. If you remain in me and my words remain in you, ask whatever you wish, and it will be given you (John 15:4-7).

The horse is made ready for the day of battle, but victory rests with the Lord (Proverbs 21:31).

Next, let's take a quick tour through the Bible to see how a few warriors applied their faith in God in life, in battle, and in victory.

GIDEON DEFEATS THE MIDIANITES

The story of Gideon defeating the Midianites (Judges 7:1-25) is one of the most profound examples of faith in the Bible.

> Early in the morning, Gideon and all his men camped at the spring of Harod. The camp of Midian was north of them in the valley near the hill of Moreh. The Lord said to Gideon, "You have too many men for me to deliver Midian into their hands. In order that Israel may not boast against me that her own strength has saved her, announce now to the people, 'Anyone who trembles with fear may turn back and leave Mount Gilead.'" So twenty-two thousand men left, while ten thousand remained.
>
> But the Lord said to Gideon, "There are still too many men. Take them down to the water, and I will sift them for you there. If I say, 'This one shall go with you,' he shall go; but if I say, 'This one shall not go with you,' he shall not go."
>
> So Gideon took the men down to the water. There the Lord told him, "Separate those who lap the water with their tongues like a dog from those who kneel down to drink." Three hundred men lapped with their hands to their mouths. All the rest got down on their knees to drink.
>
> The Lord said to Gideon, "With the three hundred men that lapped I will save you and give the Midianites into your hands. Let all the other men go, each to his own place." So Gideon sent the rest of the Israelites to their tents but kept the three

hundred, who took over the provisions and trumpets of the others.

Now the camp of Midian lay below him in the valley. During that night the Lord said to Gideon, "Get up, go down against the camp, because I am going to give it into your hands. If you are afraid to attack, go down to the camp with your servant Purah and listen to what they are saying. Afterward, you will be encouraged to attack the camp." So he and Purah his servant went down to the outposts of the camp. The Midianites, the Amalekites and all the other eastern peoples had settled in the valley, thick as locusts. Their camels could no more be counted than the sand on the seashore.

Gideon arrived just as a man was telling a friend his dream. "I had a dream," he was saying. "A round loaf of barley bread came tumbling into the Midianite camp. It struck the tent with such force that the tent overturned and collapsed."

His friend responded, "This can be nothing other than the sword of Gideon son of Joash, the Israelite. God has given the Midianites and the whole camp into his hands."

When Gideon heard the dream and its interpretation, he worshipped God. He returned to the camp of Israel and called out, "Get up! The Lord has given the Midianite camp into your hands." Dividing the three hundred men into three companies, he placed trumpets and empty jars in the hands of all of them, with torches inside.

"Watch me," he told them. "Follow my lead. When I get to the edge of the camp, do exactly as I do. When I and all who are with me blow our trumpets, then from all around the camp blow yours and shout, 'For the Lord and for Gideon.'"

Gideon and the hundred men with him reached the edge of the camp at the beginning of the middle watch, just after they had changed the guard. They blew their trumpets and broke the jars that were in their hands. The three companies blew the trumpets and smashed the jars. Grasping the torches in their left hands and holding in their right hands the trumpets they were to blow, they shouted, "A sword for the Lord and for Gideon!" While each man held his position around the camp, all the Midianites ran, crying out as they fled.

When the three hundred trumpets sounded, the Lord caused the men throughout the camp to turn on each other with their swords. The army fled to Beth Shittah toward Zererah as far as the border of Abel Meholah near Tabbath. Israelites from Naphtali, Asher, and all Manasseh were called out, and they pursued the Midianites. Gideon sent messengers throughout the hill country of Ephraim, saying, "Come down against the Midianites and seize the waters of the Jordan ahead of them as far as Beth Barah."

So all the men of Ephraim were called out and they took the waters of the Jordan as far as Beth Barah. They also captured two of the Midianite leaders, Oreb and Zeeb. They killed Oreb at the rock of Oreb, and Zeeb at the winepress of Zeeb. They

pursued the Midianites and brought the heads of
Oreb and Zeeb to Gideon, who was by the Jordan.

Imagine—God reduced his army from thirty-two thousand to
only three hundred so that Gideon would have faith in God's victory
and so "Israel may not boast against me that her own strength has
saved her." Then, God said, "If you are [still] afraid to attack, go
down to the camp with your servant Purah and listen to what they
are saying. Afterward, you will be encouraged to attack the camp."
As if that was not enough, God allowed Gideon to defeat an entire
army of Midianites without even using their conventional weapons!
Rather, God brought victory through breaking jars and torches . . .
something I am sure they never learned in hand-to-hand combat
training. And still, as if that was not enough, God "caused the men
throughout the camp to turn on each other with their swords" so
Gideon did not even have to fight the battle! All that was left for
Gideon to do was to chase down the remnants of the fleeing army
and bring the heads of their leaders back to camp. Gideon had faith
in God, and it was immediately rewarded.

DAVID AND GOLIATH

Chances are you have probably heard the story of David and Goliath.
But let's take another look.

> He looked David over and saw that he was only a
> boy, ruddy and handsome, and he despised him.
> He said to David, "Am I a dog, that you come at
> me with sticks?" And the Philistine cursed David
> by his gods. "Come here," he said, "and I'll give
> your flesh to the birds of the air and the beasts of
> the field!" David said to the Philistine, "You come
> against me with sword and spear and javelin, but I
> come against you in the name of the Lord Almighty,
> the God of the armies of Israel, whom you have

defied. This day the Lord will hand you over to me, and I'll strike you down and cut off your head. Today I will give the carcasses of the Philistine army to the birds of the air and the beasts of the earth, and the whole world will know that there is a God in Israel. All those gathered here will know that it is not by sword or spear that the Lord saves; for the battle is the Lord's, and he will give all of you into our hands." As the Philistine moved closer to attack him, David *ran quickly toward the battle line to meet him* (1 Samuel 17:42-48, emphasis added).

Did you catch that? You just read about how a humble, small, ruddy, teenage boy told a nine-foot giant that he was going to "strike [him] down and cut off [his] head." And as if that was not enough, he added that he would give the giant's carcass "to the birds of the air." Did David say these fighting words because he was a cocky, inexperienced, young teenager? No, quite the contrary. He said them because the giant was opposed to the living God of heaven and because David had completely invested his faith in God. He said it so that "all those gathered" would know that it was "not by sword or spear that the Lord saves; for the battle is the Lord's, and he will give all of you into our hands."

FISHING WITH JESUS

Luke unveils a less gory story of faith in his gospel, which he describes as follows:

One day as Jesus was standing by the Lake of Gennesaret, with the people crowding around him and listening to the word of God, he saw at the water's edge two boats, left there by the fishermen, who were washing their nets. He got into one of the boats, the one belonging to Simon, and asked him to put out a little from shore. Then he sat down and taught the people from the boat. When he had finished speaking, he said to Simon, "Put out into deep water, and let down the nets for a catch." Simon answered, "Master, we've worked hard all night and haven't caught anything. *But because you say so*, I will let down the nets" (Luke 5:1-5, emphasis added).

Imagine Simon (later called Peter)—an experienced and seasoned fisherman—being told by Jesus to go back "out into deep water, and let down the nets for a catch." They had just returned from a fishing trip. They were all wrapped up—even washing the nets and putting the other equipment away. *Then* Jesus tells them to go back out. What humility and patience it must have taken for Simon to go back out into deep water and fish again that day. But he did, and he was blessed by his obedience, for they caught so many fish that "their nets began to break" (v. 6). A true knight obeys God and trusts Him for the outcome. True faith is acting on God's ways and promises, *even when they do not make sense or feel good* (see Proverbs 3:5-6).

JOAN OF ARC

When Joan of Arc believed that she had received instruction from God, she acted. Consider this example:

Joan was just starting an afternoon rest, when suddenly she sprang up, waking her squire, Jean de Metz. "In God's name, my counsel has told me I must attack the English." She wasn't sure where she should go, but quickly arming, she called for her horse and spurred it toward the Burgundy Gate. She heard someone say the enemy was doing great harm to the French, and indeed Joan could see the Frenchmen running back to the city, some wounded and bleeding. Without alerting Joan, Dunois had launched an attack on the English fortifications at St. Loup, not quite two miles east of the city. The French were getting the worst of it and were in full retreat when Joan appeared. Seeing her with her white standard [banner] raised on high, the French gave cheer, turned back to the assault, and pressed on with such force that the English suddenly yielded. St. Loup was taken, and the palisades surrounding it were burned to the ground. One hundred fourteen English lay dead, and forty were taken prisoner. Though not a big battle, this was an important victory. It was the first time in a long siege that the French had captured an English fort. Had the French lost, the English surely would have gone on to capture the Burgundy Gate and to seal off Orleans completely.[14]

Most knights in today's world will not exercise their faith by defeating the Midianites, slinging rocks at giants, going fishing with Jesus, or launching attacks against English fortifications. But our daily battles are just as critical and real in God's eyes. God personally asked Gideon to reduce his army and trust more in Him. God filled and used the shell of a young man to defeat a giant warrior, but David himself carried out the act. Jesus, our very personal Lord, asked Peter eye-to-eye to throw the net on the other side of the boat. God pleads with us to rely on Him and trust.

REFLECT

The horse is made ready for the day of battle, but victory rests with the Lord.

—Proverbs 21:31

Some trust in chariots and some in horses, but we trust in the name of the Lord our God. They are brought to their knees and fall, but we rise up and stand firm.

—Psalm 20:7-8

Yet I will show love to the house of Judah; and I will save them—not by bow, sword, or battle, or by horses and horsemen, but by the Lord their God.

—Hosea 1:7

A knight without faith may not possess good habits of life, for by faith a man sees God and His works spiritually and believes in the invisible things. By faith, a man is enabled to have hope, charity, and loyalty and becomes a servant of honesty and truth. Lacking faith, a man will not believe in God's Incarnation, nor in His works or the things that he cannot directly see—which a man without faith may not understand nor know. Knights whose habits are shaped by faith often go into the land beyond the sea on pilgrimage and there prove their strength and knighthood against the enemies of the Cross and become martyrs if they die. For they fight to uphold the Holy Christian Faith. Also, on account of faith, clerics are defended by Knights from wicked men who, through fraud, rob and disinherit them insofar as possible.[15]

—Ramon Lull

The Knight who has no faith and practices no faith and opposes them who defend it is like a man to whom God has given reason but who pursues foolishness.[16]

—Ramon Lull

RESPOND

1. How is faith a form of trust?
2. Who are you trusting in your life? Do you have misplaced trust in someone or something?
3. How can we build more trust in God?
4. Why is faith so important for a knight?
5. How will faith benefit your life in the short run? In the long run?

HOPE

> Let us not become weary in doing good, for at the proper time we will reap a harvest if we do not give up. Therefore, as we have opportunity, let us do good to all people, especially to those who belong to the family of believers.
>
> —Galatians 6:9-10
>
> Even youths grow tired and weary, and young men stumble and fall; but those who hope in the LORD will renew their strength. They will soar on wings like eagles; they will run and not grow weary, they will walk and not be faint.
>
> —Isaiah 40:30-31

Wikipedia defines *hope* as "The emotional state, the opposite of which is despair, which promotes the belief in a positive outcome related to events and circumstances in one's life."[17] Throughout Scripture, we are presented with passages that inspire us to hope in God and not ourselves or some other external resource or power:

> His pleasure is not in the strength of the horse, nor
> his delight in the legs of a man; the Lord delights

in those who fear him, who put their hope in his unfailing love (Psalm 147:10-11).

Wait for the Lord. Be strong and take heart and wait for the Lord (Psalm 27:14).

Some trust in chariots and some in horses, but we trust in the name of the Lord our God (Psalm 20:7).

Hope really comes down to what you actually believe in when the chips are on the table. One Old Testament story (2 Chronicles 32) shows what can happen when a leader is faced with an "all in" situation and chooses to hope only in God.

The year was 701 BC, and the leader of God's people, King Hezekiah, was cornered by Sennacherib, the king of Assyria. Sennacherib was invading King Hezekiah's homeland (Judah) and was getting ready to annihilate God's people and add Judah to his growing list of real estate. He had already laid siege to the surrounding fortified cities and was getting ready to make war on Jerusalem.

When Hezekiah saw that Sennacherib had turned his forces on Jerusalem, he made preparations for war and started a counter-strategy by blocking off the water from the springs outside the city so the king of Assyria would not have access to the water supply. Then, right before the battle with the Assyrian army was upon them, he gathered his military officers and encouraged them with these words: "'Be strong and courageous. Do not be afraid or discouraged because of the king of Assyria and the vast army with him, for there is a greater power with us than with him. With him is only the arm of flesh, but with us is the Lord our God to help us and to fight our battles.' And the people gained confidence from what Hezekiah the king of Judah said" (32:7-8). Hezekiah gave them weapons, shields, an offensive strategy (blocking off the water), and then he gave them the best asset in battle—he gave them *hope*.

So what happened next? Were God's people disappointed? No. They trusted in God and watched the truth of this verse unfold before their very eyes: "No one whose hope is in you will ever be put to shame, but they will be put to shame who are treacherous without excuse" (Psalm 25:3).

But not without a challenge first. While King Sennacherib was attacking a neighboring city, he sent his officers to Jerusalem with a message specifically designed to destroy the hope of God's people. The message was addressed to both King Hezekiah and all the people of Judah: "On what are you basing your confidence, that you remain in Jerusalem under siege? When Hezekiah says, 'The Lord our God will save us from the hand of the king of Assyria,' he is misleading you, to let you die of hunger and thirst" (2 Chronicles 32:10-11). So now King Hezekiah and the people had a choice: Believe and hope in God, or look at their circumstances and believe the threat of the enemy that they would die of hunger and thirst.

The Bible records their choice—they prayed and put their hope in God. "King Hezekiah and the prophet Isaiah son of Amoz cried out in prayer to heaven about this" (32:20). What happens next is simply amazing. They did not even need to fight in the battle. The Lord saw their trust, sent a heavenly angel who completely wiped out the entire fighting force of the Assyrian army, including their leaders. And what happened to King Sennacherib? He withdrew to his own land in disgrace. And when he finally arrived home, he entered the temple of his (false) god, and some of his sons rushed him and cut him down with swords (32:21). God wins.

The well-known story of David and Goliath reflects a similar situation: an under-equipped and overwhelmed child of God faced with a spiritual decision—who to place his hope in. David could have put his hope in his brothers, the Israelite army, the armor of Saul, or the five rocks he took from the creek bed for ammunition. But he did not. David put his hope fully in God:

> David said to the Philistine, "You come against me
> with sword and spear and javelin, but I come against

> you in the name of the Lord Almighty, the God of
> the armies of Israel, whom you have defied. This day
> the Lord will hand you over to me, and I'll strike
> you down and cut off your head. Today I will give
> the carcasses of the Philistine army to the birds of
> the air and the beasts of the earth, and the whole
> world will know that there is a God in Israel" (1
> Samuel 17:45-46).

In life, we can wait, hope, and trust in God or act in our own feeble efforts and waste our time and energy. Hoping in God means holding steadfast and taking action *when and how* he prompts us. My personal story that follows shows that having hope can also mean staying the course and waiting for God's best in our lives.

When I was about eighteen years old, my friend Peter and I were out on a Friday night, tracking down whatever fun the nightlife could offer two young and reckless men. We ran into a few young ladies that night who were also up to no good. Just before chasing into a night that could have ended in sin, I drove home to pick up a few things. While walking through the kitchen, I muttered something to my mom like, "I'm tired of waiting for God's choice for a woman in my life. I'm going to go find my own now." While storming past her on my way out the door, she said, "That's fine, Danny. Just remember that Esau gave up his entire birthright for a bowl of stew." Then she just turned and went back to bed. It was like she had tied a rope around my ankles and jerked my feet out from under me. I hung my motorcycle keys by the door and went to bed.

The passage my mom referenced that night was Genesis 25:29-34:

> Once when Jacob was cooking some stew, Esau
> came in from the open country, famished. He said
> to Jacob, "Quick, let me have some of that red stew!
> I'm famished!" Jacob replied, "First sell me your
> birthright." "Look, I am about to die," Esau said.

"What good is the birthright to me?" But Jacob said, "Swear to me first." So he swore an oath to him, selling his birthright to Jacob. Then Jacob gave Esau some bread and some lentil stew. He ate and drank, and then got up and left. So Esau despised his birthright.

All can be lost without hope. Hope is really the only way one can move beyond bad choices and make good ones; the only way one can overlook temptations in exchange for future blessings. Real rewards await those who choose wisely. Had I gone out that night, full of mischievous ambition, there's a good chance I would not have had the life, wife, and kids I have now. When my hope was almost gone, it was the last glimmer of my future that my mom showed me that helped me stay the course.

REFLECT

For I know the plans I have for you," declares the Lord, "plans to prosper you and not to harm you, plans to give you hope and a future.

—Jeremiah 29:11

Yet this I call to mind and therefore I have hope: Because of the Lord's great love we are not consumed, for his compassions never fail. They are new every morning; great is your faithfulness. I say to myself, "The Lord is my portion; therefore I will wait for him. The Lord is good to those whose hope is in him, to the one who seeks him."

—Lamentations 3:21-25

Know also that wisdom is sweet to your soul; if you find it, there is a future hope for you, and your hope will not be cut off.

—Proverbs 24:14

Hope in God. If you have good hope and faith in him, you shall be delivered from your enemies.

—Joan of Arc[18]

RESPOND

1. King Hezekiah hoped in God, but he still prepared weapons and took strategic action. How can we do both in our lives—trust God *and* act?
2. In difficult situations, we are faced with the choice between hoping and despairing. What practical ways can we choose hope and avoid despair?
3. How can hoping in God's best save our time and resources?
4. What happens if we trust in ourselves rather than in God?
5. How did King Hezekiah give his followers hope? How can you follow his example when giving hope to others in your life?
6. How does hope empower us to overcome temptation?
7. How does a modern-day knight cultivate hope?
8. What role does worship play in keeping us hoping for a better day?

LOVE

Therefore, as God's chosen people, holy and dearly loved, clothe yourselves with compassion, kindness, humility, gentleness, and patience. Bear with each other and forgive whatever grievances you may have against one another. Forgive as the Lord forgave you, and over all these virtues put on love, which binds them all together in perfect unity.

—Colossians 3:12-14

Love—not gallantry or pride—should drive a knight to be a knight and should govern his thoughts and actions. Before even looking into this virtue, let's first start with the very definition of love provided by Scripture:

> Love is patient, love is kind. It does not envy, it does not boast, it is not proud. It is not rude, it is not self-seeking, it is not easily angered, it keeps no record of wrongs. Love does not delight in evil but rejoices with the truth. It always protects, always trusts, always hopes, always perseveres. Love never fails (1 Corinthians 13:4-8).

Do you notice the knightly virtues in this passage? Patience, kindness, humility, seeking the best for others, forgiveness, truth-seeking, protection, trust, hope, and perseverance. All of these are knightly virtues.

Why are these traits important? They are important because *you waste your life if you do not live by them*:

> If I speak in the tongues of men and of angels, but have not love, I am only a resounding gong or a clanging cymbal. If I have the gift of prophecy and can fathom all mysteries and all knowledge, and if I have a faith that can move mountains, but have not love, I am nothing. If I give all I possess to the poor and surrender my body to the flames, but have not love, I gain nothing (1 Corinthians 13:1-3).

Without love, your knightly life, virtue, and deeds are worthless. According to the passage above, without love, your life is reduced to a clanging symbol, you *are nothing*, and you can *gain nothing*. For these reasons, a true knight lives with love as his life's main goal. All of his actions should come from a place of love—especially, those actions that require defending others in the heat of battle.

How can this be done? How can a knight love others? Consider this: In order to share the love of Christ with others, one must first experience it. We must first understand that we are loved and forgiven. The gospel of John is sometimes called the Gospel of Love because even the very first chapter explains in no uncertain terms that we are loved by God as *individuals*: "Yet to all who received him, to those who believed in his name, he gave the right to become children of God—children born not of natural descent, nor of human decision or a husband's will, but born of God" (1:12-13). Put simply, our belief and faith in Christ gives us the right to become children of God. He adopts us when we believe in Him unconditionally and fully, without reservation. And it is through this faith in Him that we receive grace and acceptance from the Creator of the Universe:

"Therefore, since we have been justified through faith, we have peace with God through our Lord Jesus Christ, through whom we have gained access by faith into this grace in which we now stand" (Romans 5:1-2).

After we get this first part straight and understand it with the simplicity and wholeheartedness of a child (Mark 10:15), we can then share it with others. By knowing and feeling that we are unconditionally loved and accepted as adopted children of God, His grace and forgiveness flows from our lives and encourages us to love and forgive others. Just as Christ works with us and through us despite our shortcomings and weaknesses, we must bear with others: "We who are strong ought to bear with the failings of the weak and not to please ourselves" (Romans 15:1), and "Carry each other's burdens, and in this way you will fulfill the law of Christ" (Galatians 6:2).

Finally, we show our love for others by our forgiveness: "Therefore, if you are offering your gift at the altar and there remember that your brother has something against you, leave your gift there in front of the altar. First go and be reconciled to your brother; then come and offer your gift" (Matthew 5:23-24).

REFLECT

Be imitators of God, therefore, as dearly loved children and live a life of love, just as Christ loved us and gave himself up for us as a fragrant offering and sacrifice to God.

—Ephesians 5:1-2

We who are strong ought to bear with the failings of the weak and not to please ourselves.

—Romans 15:1

If you really keep the royal law found in Scripture, "Love your neighbor as yourself," you are doing right.

—James 2:8

Respond

1. Why is it important that God loves us first?
2. What does it mean to "bear with" others?
3. When do we *confront* others in love, and when do we *overlook* and "bear with" others?
4. Why is love a knightly trait and not a trait for wimps?
5. Why is hatred, gossip, and cruelty easier than love?

JUSTICE

> Good will come to him who is generous and lends freely, who conducts his affairs with justice. Surely he will never be shaken; a righteous man will be remembered forever. He will have no fear of bad news; his heart is steadfast, trusting in the LORD. His heart is secure, he will have no fear; in the end he will look in triumph on his foes.
>
> —Psalm 112:5-8
>
> He has showed you, O man, what is good. And what does the LORD require of you? To act justly and to love mercy and to walk humbly with your God.
>
> —Micah 6:8

Reverend Tim Keller authored an entire book on the concept of Christian justice, *Generous Justice: How God's Grace Makes Us Just*. When interviewed[19] about this work and asked to provide a summary definition of justice, Reverend Keller said, "Caring for the vulnerable." He also provided an umbrella definition of justice: "Giving people what they deserve." While that definition can have a negative tone (i.e., finding and stopping evildoers), he described a positive aspect as well: "Looking to the vulnerable—to people made in the image of God—and asking ourselves: 'Are they getting the kind of *care* they're due? As beings made in God's image, are they being cared for properly?'" He then boils down justice to this: "Giving people what they are due. So we punish evildoers, and we care for the vulnerable." This is a very tight definition for a very complex issue.

Many might believe that applying the concepts of justice in modern times is limited to only those who work in the criminal justice system. But that's not the case. Modern knights living in virtually any life situation can work to uphold justice. Ethically practicing justice in all things great and small should be important to your life because they are important to God. It does not matter if you are lobbying to create or uphold laws that are just or dividing up cookies between your kids, for God desires each of us to apply justice within our sphere of influence and within the race He calls us to run.

Ramon Lull believed that justice is fundamentally intertwined with knighthood:

> If a man without justice were a Knight, it would follow that justice would not be in that place where in fact it is, and that knighthood would be something altogether different from what it is. Nor is it relevant that a Knight may have a smattering of justice and believes himself to be in the Order of Knighthood—if he is, in truth, injurious, he doesn't belong at all. For knighthood and justice are so intimately intertwined that knighthood cannot survive without justice. An injurious Knight is an enemy to justice and defeats and expels himself from the Order.

Scripture reveals that God *loves* justice ("For the Lord is righteous, he loves justice; upright men will see his face" (Psalm 11:7)) and that justice is the *foundation* of his throne ("Righteousness and justice are the foundation of your throne; love and faithfulness go before you" (Psalm 89:14)). Not only is justice the concrete that makes up the foundation of God's throne, those who live by it are promised blessing: "Blessed are they who maintain justice, who constantly do what is right" (Psalm 106:3). We are given a promise in Scripture that if we seek the Lord, we will fully understand God's definition of justice: "Evil men do not understand justice, but those who seek the Lord understand it fully" (Proverbs 28:5).

Sometimes living justly can include actively working to establish and uphold justice as well as loosening the chains of injustice:

- **ESTABLISHING AND UPHOLDING JUSTICE:**

  o By justice a king gives a country stability, but one who is greedy for bribes tears it down (Proverbs 29:4).

  o To fear the Lord is to hate evil; I [Wisdom] hate pride and arrogance, evil behavior, and perverse speech. Counsel and sound judgment are mine; I have understanding and power. By me kings reign and rulers make laws that are just; by me princes govern, and all nobles who rule on earth (Proverbs 8:13-16).

- **LOOSING THE CHAINS OF INJUSTICE:**

  o "Is not this the kind of fasting I have chosen: to *loose the chains of injustice* and untie the cords of the yoke, to set the oppressed free and break every yoke? Is it not to share your food with the hungry and to provide the poor wanderer with shelter—when you see the naked, to clothe him, and not to turn away from your own flesh and blood? Then your light will break forth like the dawn, and your healing will quickly appear; then your righteousness will go before you, and the glory of the Lord will be your rear guard" (Isaiah 58:6-8).

Believe it or not, God will give you several opportunities to exercise justice in both these ways of establishing justice and preventing injustice.

REFLECT

To administer justice badly or to neglect the customs that are most essential to his knightly duty is simply to despise the Order itself; therefore, as all these things aforementioned concern a Knight's physical preparedness, so justice, wisdom, charity, loyalty, truth, humility, strength, hope, promptness and all other similar virtues pertain to the preparedness of the Knight's soul.

—Ramon Lull

If a Knight is consumed with pride and seeks by that means to uphold the Order of Knighthood, he is in fact corrupting it, for his Order was founded on justice and humility with a view to protecting the humble against the proud."

—Ramon Lull

RESPOND

1. How can a modern-day knight fight injustice?
2. How can a modern-day knight establish justice?
3. How can a modern-day knight uphold justice?
4. Why is justice important to God?
5. How do we actively pursue justice?

VIRTUE 6

PRUDENCE

> Therefore be careful how you walk, not as unwise men but as wise, making the most of your time, because the days are evil. So then do not be foolish, but understand what the will of the Lord is.
>
> —Ephesians 5:15-17 (ASV)
>
> Whoever can be trusted with very little can also be trusted with much, and whoever is dishonest with very little will also be dishonest with much. So if you have not been trustworthy in handling worldly wealth, who will trust you with true riches? And if you have not been trustworthy with someone else's property, who will give you property of your own?
>
> —Luke 16:10-12

In the time of the medieval knight, taking prudent action made the difference between life and death, wealth or poverty, health or illness, safety or turmoil, marriage or no marriage, and children or no children. And it is no different for today's knight. Making prudent decisions daily will help lead to a fruitful and effective life. So what is prudence? The Webster dictionary defines *prudence* as:

- the ability to govern and discipline oneself by the use of reason;

- sagacity or shrewdness in the management of affairs;
- skill and good judgment in the use of resources; and
- caution or circumspection as to danger or risk.[20]

There is a "million dollar" word in the definition above—*sagacious*. Sagacious is defined as "keen in sense perception" and "of keen and farsighted penetration and judgment."[21] Take a moment to look at this part of prudence because it is truly a characteristic that can differentiate someone's life. Many young men and women today are not living their lives by applying "farsighted penetration and judgment." Rather, many live their lives by shortsightedness and poor judgment and allow impulses and desires to set their priorities rather than planning prudent and wise steps to develop their future. If you are a woman, please read Proverbs 31 for God's definition of a prudent, godly woman. Prudence is by far the dominant theme in the entire chapter.

Acting out of prudence means basing your decisions on where your twenty-year-old self wants your thirty-year-old self to be in ten years, or the thirties to the forties, fifties to sixties, etc. Every day should be invested, not just lived. There are so many distractions in life that take us away from this reality, stealing our future by stealing our days with fruitless deeds and obsessions.

To help make one's life as productive as possible, let's explore three aspects of living a life based on prudence: (1) planning, (2) focus, and (3) hard work with perseverance.

PLANNING

Consider the following verses from Proverbs about the importance of planning:

> Every prudent man acts out of knowledge, but a
> fool exposes his folly (13:16).

The wisdom of the prudent is to give thought to their ways, but the folly of fools is deception (14:8).

It is not good to have zeal without knowledge, nor to be hasty and miss the way (19:2).

The plans of the diligent lead to profit as surely as haste leads to poverty (21:5).

Planning occurs when we take time before *doing* the work to *plan* the work so it can be done correctly and efficiently. Planning is where we apply the carpenter's rule: measure twice; cut only once. We honor God by intentionally and deliberately going about the work to which He has called us. Sometimes this means getting up a little earlier; sometimes it means working late. But planning is the way that we make sure the *right thing is done in the right way.*

A skillful modern knight goes before his or her team to plan a project in advance. By doing so, he or she honors the time of the followers by making sure their work is done effectively and efficiently. Perhaps the best example of this was Nehemiah. The walls around Jerusalem were broken down, and he had received permission from the king of Babylon to rebuild them. However, before he or anyone else fitted a single stone to the new wall, he surveyed the work to be done, and he did this quietly, prayerfully and deliberately.

I set out during the night with a few men. I had not told anyone what my God had put in my heart to do for Jerusalem. There were no mounts with me except the one I was riding on. By night I went out through the Valley Gate . . . examining the walls of Jerusalem, which had been broken down, and its gates, which had been destroyed by fire. Then I moved on toward the Fountain Gate and the King's Pool, but there was not enough room for my mount to get through; so I went up the valley

37

by night, examining the wall. Finally, I turned back
and reentered through the Valley Gate. The officials
did not know where I had gone or what I was doing,
because as yet *I had said nothing to the Jews or the
priests or nobles or officials or any others who would
be doing the work* (Nehemiah 2:12-16, emphasis
added).

Nehemiah did this planning work quietly and unannounced. He
did it with only a few men and limited resources.

FOCUS

Focus is the next key element we will consider. The following verses
from Proverbs speak to the importance of *focus*:

He who works his land will have abundant food, but
he who chases fantasies lacks judgment (12:11).

All hard work brings a profit, but mere talk leads
only to poverty (14:23).

I have enjoyed the sport of archery throughout the years. For
birthdays, family gatherings, and holidays, we typically have several
children and adventurous adults try out their archery skills in a
range in our backyard. After watching and training people over the
years, I have formed the opinion that there are two types of archers:
those who shoot arrows downrange, and those who *really aim* before
shooting—those who want to pierce the bull's-eye so badly they can
feel it in their bones.

Our good family friend, Max, falls into the second category of
shooters—the type who can almost feel the path of the arrow or
bullet to the bull's-eye. About a year ago, I took Max to the shooting
range where we could try our focus using an old-fashioned buffalo
rifle (an 1874 Sharps in 45-70 caliber). After we each warmed up

with several practice shots, we took aim at a fresh target set at one hundred yards. I was lucky enough to hit the bull's-eye on the first shot, making a clean hole right in the middle. Next, I handed the rifle to Max who then did the impossible—he shot a bullet *right through my bullet hole*, cutting it only slightly larger on all sides. Amazed, I later gave him the target set in a picture frame. Now that's *focus*!

Focus makes all the difference. It is the factor that converts your plans and perseverance into a successful outcome. Take for instance a floodlight, which casts light over a wide area. The same energy source used for a floodlight can be channeled into a laser beam that is capable of cutting through steel. That's how focus works.

HARD WORK WITH PERSEVERANCE

Hard work without follow-through will only lead to wasted efforts for many projects in life that demand staying power. Indeed, a good plan is only as good as its follow-up. Consider the following Bible verses on hard work and perseverance:

> Lazy hands make a man poor, but diligent hands bring wealth (Proverbs 10:4).

> Do not love sleep or you will grow poor; stay awake and you will have food to spare (Proverbs 20:13).

> A sluggard does not plow in season; so at harvest time he looks but finds nothing (Proverbs 20:4).

> She gets up while it is still dark; she provides food for her family and portions for her servant girls. She considers a field and buys it; out of her earnings she plants a vineyard. She sets about her work vigorously; her arms are strong for her tasks. She sees that her trading is profitable, and her lamp does not go out at night (Proverbs 31:15-18).

> Whatever your hand finds to do, do it with all your might, for in the grave, where you are going, there is neither working nor planning nor knowledge nor wisdom (Ecclesiastes 9:10).

Perseverance is the hard part. That's when we push through the difficult times by sheer force of will, relying on God's promise: "I can do all things through Christ who strengthens me (Philippians 4:13). Pushing happens when we work *even when we do not want to*. This means getting out of bed when you do not want to and putting in another day—even after all the inspiration and enthusiasm is gone. My mother referred to perseverance as "stick-to-itiveness."

Working hard is actually the easy way of doing work because it takes less effort than being lazy in the long run. By "putting your elbows into it" rather than slowly mushing your way through the day's work, you will get your work done much faster and leave more time for rest and recuperation. The Lord knows what your best looks like, and He wants all of it.

The Ways in which a Knight can Apply Prudence

A knight's love for others leads him to want to help others financially; his prudence guides him how to do so wisely.

A knight's strength leads him to help others carry their burdens in life; his prudence reminds him to rest at night rather than stay up late so his strength is renewed in the morning.

A knight's hope gives him expectation that a project or assignment will turn out just fine; his prudence makes him work even harder to make it come about that way.

A knight's call may lead him to battle; his prudence cautions him to seek counsel before battle (see Proverbs 20:18).

A knight's humility brings him honor; his prudence reminds him that his pride is just a thought away from dominating his heart and actions: "The heart is deceitful above all things and beyond cure. Who can understand it? I the Lord search the heart and examine the mind, to reward a man according to his conduct, according to what his deeds deserve" (Jeremiah 17:9-10).

A knight's perseverance helps him start and finish a project; his prudence teaches him to carefully plan the project so that it can be done within a reasonable time.

A knight's honor is earned by humility; only prudence can keep his honor by preserving his quality work product: "Do you see a man skilled in his work? He will serve before kings; he will not serve before obscure men" (Proverbs 22:29).

A knight's temperance in all things is only kept by his prudence in making daily decisions.

A knight's faith gives him ambition and hope; his prudence helps him forge practical ways to accomplish his goals: "Every prudent man acts out of knowledge, but a fool exposes his folly" (Proverbs 13:16).

A knight's belief in justice causes him to accept the penalty of a speeding ticket; his prudence keeps him from speeding again.

A knight's charity understands that sometimes others have need; his prudence understands that to give a man a fish, he will eat for a day, but teach a man to fish, he will eat for the rest of his life.

A knight's willingness to sacrifice himself in battle must be buffered with his prudent understanding that he must live to fight another day.

A knight's compassion leads him to want to give money to the guy on the street corner; his prudence leads him to buy him dinner instead.

A knight's loyalty to others opens his heart to friendship; his prudence gives him the understanding that friends come into our lives for a reason, a season, or a lifetime, and that he will only receive perfect loyalty from the Lord alone.

A knight's belief in truth gives light to his every step; his prudence leads him to carefully confirm teachings or rumors to find out the truth for himself: "Now the Bereans were of more noble character than the Thessalonians, for they received the message with great eagerness and examined the Scriptures every day to see if what Paul said was true" (Acts 17:11).

A knight's purity gives strength and effectiveness to his ways in the same way that Samson's vow to the Lord gave him power; his prudence leads him to understand that this strength can be sapped by walking off the path but can be restored by going back on the path.

A knight's gallantry gives him power to charge in battle wielding only a sword; his prudence teaches him to always strap a backup weapon onto his belt.

A knight's hospitality moves him to fill his home with friends; his prudence reminds him to prepare enough food.

A knight's desire to be courteous to others must be governed by his prudence, which reminds him that some people may be offended by old-fashioned chivalry.

A knight's gratitude teaches him to count his blessings; his prudence reminds him that some blessings must be earned: "Be sure you know the condition of your flocks, give careful attention to your herds; for riches do not endure forever, and a crown is not secure for all generations" (Proverbs 27:23-24).

A knight's grace and mercy gives him love, patience, and forgiveness with others; his prudence gives him caution regarding which relationships to cultivate.

A knight's prudence leads him to prepare a lesson before mentoring others.

A knight's strength will help him to overcome failure; his prudence leads him to not repeat the same mistakes twice.

REFLECT

Better a patient man than a warrior, a man who controls his temper than one who takes a city.

—Proverbs 16:32

The customs of a knight are to arm himself and to fight, but that accords not so much to the office of a knight as does the use of reason, of listening, and ordained will. For many battles have been vanquished more by mastery, by wit, and by industry than by multitudes of horsemen and good armor.

—Ramon Lull

Real rewards await those who choose wisely.

—Walt Disney

RESPOND

1. Which part of prudence is most challenging for you? Planning? Focus? Hard work?
2. Why is it important to join perseverance with focus? With planning?
3. Where does your life need more planning? More focus?
4. How can prudence benefit us in the short term? In the long term?
5. How does living a prudent life set us up for God's blessing?

VIRTUE 7

TEMPERANCE

Everything is permissible—but not everything is beneficial. Everything is permissible—but not everything is constructive. Nobody should seek his own good, but the good of others.

—1 Corinthians 10:23-24

Do not join those who drink too much wine or gorge themselves on meat, for drunkards and gluttons become poor, and drowsiness clothes them in rags.

—Proverbs 23:20-21

Temperance can be defined as "moderation in action, thought, or feeling; restraint."[22] To a knight, this means complete abstinence from some things and moderation in all things. Without this virtue, a knight's life and character will fail.

When people talk about moderation, one topic surfaces more than others—drinking alcohol. In this area, I have made a lifetime choice to abstain from alcohol. To others, occasional social drinking may be their version of moderation. Yet to others, different rules of conscience may apply. Without getting into the divisive discussion on which position is most valid, suffice it to say that all positions should include moderation. As the apostle Paul said, "Everything is permissible for me—but not everything is beneficial. Everything is permissible for me—but I will not be mastered by anything" (1 Corinthians 6:12). He also admonished that we should be more focused on being filled with the Holy Spirit than drinking in excess: "And do not get drunk with wine, for that is dissipation, but be filled with the Spirit" (Ephesians 5:18).

Whatever one's choice on the issue of drinking, a knight's strength and time is not for drunkenness or wastefulness, but for serving others:

> We who are strong ought to bear with the failings of the weak and not to please ourselves (Romans 15:1).

> Blessed are you, O land, whose king is of nobility and whose princes eat at the appropriate time— for strength and not for drunkenness (Ecclesiastes 10:17).

Temperance can also apply to things like television or social media. Allowing yourself to become obsessed with television or other drains of life and time will sap you of strength that could be used elsewhere productively. However, remember that temperance allows for reprieve and rest. Remember, because the Lord paid for your life, He owns your time too.

It is sad, but the future of many young people is being exchanged for temporary joys and pleasures like excessive video games, television, online social media, and other similar activities. Recent studies reveal that teens spend an average of sixteen hours per week online.[23] Add to this time the average time spent watching TV (another fourteen hours) and talking on the phone (another eight hours),[24] and you nearly have the same amount of time spent on a full-time job every week. Are these things bad? Are they a complete waste of time? Certainly not. But all things should be enjoyed in moderation: "Everything is permissible—but not everything is beneficial.

Everything is permissible—but not everything is constructive" (1 Corinthians 10:23).

Finally, a word of caution in the area of temperance: Be on your guard against legalism. While some personalities may be more drawn toward legalistic attitudes than others, it is certainly not an attitude endorsed by New Testament teachings (especially those from Christ Himself). Be careful not to turn others away from Christianity by judging the attitudes and behaviors of others—allow the Holy Spirit to do that work. However, if your Christian brother is caught in sin, it is your job to correct him (Galatians 6:1). Just be careful how you do it. Sometimes we can make a stronger statement by our actions rather than our words. For example, I had a good friend in high school who would excuse himself for a walk outside when the group took up smoking. His actions were not judgmental, but they were not supportive either.

REFLECT

> I rejoice greatly in the Lord that at last you have renewed your concern for me. Indeed, you have been concerned, but you had no opportunity to show it. I am not saying this because I am in need, for I have learned to be content whatever the circumstances. I know what it is to be in need, and I know what it is to have plenty. I have learned the secret of being content in any and every situation, whether well fed or hungry, whether living in plenty or in want. I can do everything through him who gives me strength.
>
> —Philippians 4:10-13

RESPOND

1. How can one live along the fine line between excess, or indulgence, and legalism?

2. What may be acceptable for you as a Christian may not be acceptable to another. In these gray areas (where Scripture does not call the behavior a clear sin), how can you live with grace and be accepting of others?
3. Is it ever our job to suggest temperance in the life of another believer? Of a non-Christian?
4. In what areas of your life do you need to apply temperance?
5. How can applying the trait of temperance make our lives more enjoyable?

VIRTUE 8

STRENGTH

> No king is saved by the size of his army; no warrior escapes by his great strength. A horse is a vain hope for deliverance; despite all its great strength it cannot save. But the eyes of the LORD are on those who fear him, on those whose hope is in his unfailing love, to deliver them from death and keep them alive in famine. We wait in hope for the LORD; He is our help and our shield.
>
> —Psalm 33:16-20

Scripture and the world alike define knightly traits like honesty almost identically. Honesty just is what it is. This is not so, however, with the knightly trait of strength. In fact, Scripture and the world define *strength* in quite opposite ways. Let me explain.

If we are "full of ourselves," we are usually not "full of God." Being empowered and acting out of our own self-will and drive will usually not get us very far, at least not in God's eyes. God prefers us to be emptied of our own strength and ready to be filled with His strength. When wrestling with the issue of strength, the apostle Paul asked God three times to remove a thorn in his side that was sapping him of his energy and stamina. God refused to remove it, however, and instead said to Paul, "My grace is sufficient for you, for my power is made perfect in weakness" (2 Corinthians 12:9). Paul goes on to write, "Therefore I will boast all the more gladly about my weaknesses, so that Christ's power may rest on me. That is why, for Christ's sake, I delight in weaknesses, in insults, in hardships, in persecutions, in difficulties. For when I am weak, then I am strong" (2 Corinthians 12:10). There we have it—our weakness clears the way for God's strength to *rest on us*. Next, let's turn to just how we can be filled with such strength.

Jesus: The Source of Real Strength

Christ says that if we drink from the waters of this world, we will continue to thirst. In other words, if we draw our strength from the wells of the world, we will continue to need this source for our strength. The world offers many such wells—wealth, fame, hobbies, and many interests that, when out of balance in our lives, can become wells that leave us thirsty.

But if we drink from the water that Christ gives, we will not only plug the hole in the bottom of our souls, Christ Himself will cause a new spring of living water to well up from *within* us. When Jesus was speaking with a Samaritan woman at a well, He asked her for a drink of water. She replied, "You are a Jew, and I am a Samaritan woman. How can you ask me for a drink?" His response to her was amazing:

Jesus answered her, "If you knew the gift of God and who it is that asks you for a drink, you would have asked him and he would have given you living water." "Sir," the woman said, "you have nothing to draw with and the well is deep. Where can you get this living water? Are you greater than our father Jacob, who gave us the well and drank from it himself, as did also his sons and his flocks and herds?" Jesus answered, "Everyone who drinks this water will be thirsty again, but whoever drinks the water I give him will never thirst. Indeed, the water I give him will become in him a spring of water welling up to eternal life" (John 4:10-14).

This concept of sourcing your well of inner strength with the Lord is also mentioned in the Old Testament:

> As they make music they will sing, "All my fountains are in you" (Psalms 87:7).

> They feast on the abundance of your house; you give them drink from your river of delights. For with you is the fountain of life; in your light we see light (Psalm 36:8-9).

> My people have committed two sins: They have forsaken me, the spring of living water, and have dug their own cisterns, broken cisterns that cannot hold water (Jeremiah 2:13).

The verse from Jeremiah above shows what can happen to our strength if our hearts are *not* tapped into the Lord. If we dig our own cisterns—our own sources of encouragement, support, and strength—they will eventually leak, leaving us emptier than when we started relying on them. What is sapping your strength? Are you digging any empty, broken wells in your life? Let God redirect you to the *living* well.

STRENGTH IN THE LIFE OF A MODERN KNIGHT

While still very important, a modern knight's need for strength to survive battles is no longer physical but spiritual—dealing with a person's will. Let me explain. Have you ever experienced a situation where you felt weak at the knees? Could hardly talk? Have you ever trembled in fear? Have you ever felt like someone or something knocked the wind right out of your chest, all without even being physically touched? I certainly have. If you haven't yet, live long enough and you will (it is a certainty!).

However these challenges come, we need to be ready for them. Unfortunately, there are no recipes for whipping up superhuman strength when these situations arise. But here comes the caveat—while we cannot control how our bodies may physically or emotionally respond when we experience shock or fright, we can load up on physical, spiritual, and emotional strength to be prepared for when these situations occur. True strength comes only from God and through our dependence on God:

> Once you spoke in a vision, to your faithful people you said: "I have bestowed strength on a warrior; I have exalted a young man from among the people. I have found David my servant; with my sacred oil I have anointed him. My hand will sustain him; surely my arm will strengthen him. No enemy will subject him to tribute; no wicked man will oppress him. I will crush his foes before him and strike down his adversaries. My faithful love will be with him, and through my name his horn will be exalted" (Psalm 89:19-24).

> Even youths grow tired and weary, and young men stumble and fall; but those who hope in the Lord will renew their strength. They will soar on wings like eagles; they will run and not grow weary, they will walk and not be faint (Isaiah 40:30-31).

> For to be sure, he was crucified in weakness, yet he lives by God's power. Likewise, we are weak in him, yet by God's power we will live with him to serve you (2 Corinthians 13:4).

> To keep me [the apostle Paul] from becoming conceited because of these surpassingly great revelations, there was given me a thorn in my flesh,

a messenger of Satan, to torment me. Three times I pleaded with the Lord to take it away from me. But he said to me, "My grace is sufficient for you, for my power is made perfect in weakness." Therefore I will boast all the more gladly about my weaknesses, so that Christ's power may rest on me. That is why, for Christ's sake, I delight in weaknesses, in insults, in hardships, in persecutions, in difficulties. For when I am weak, then I am strong (2 Corinthians 12:7-10).

There are some major differences between the strength of a worldly knight or warrior compared to God's knight. Some of these are provided in the table below.

Challenge	The World's Knight is . . .	God's Knight is . . .
Discouragement	Self-reliant	Encouraged by God, the Bible, and the counsel of others
Hitting a road block	Determined and stubborn	Surrendered and determined
A competitive situation	Driven by pride	Driven by a desire to please God
Abundance	Used for personal gain	Purposefully used for the benefit of others
Failure	Compelled to "pull himself up by the bootstraps"	Seeks God through prayer and waits on the Lord
Injustice that involves the loss of personal pride	Compelled to take revenge	Inclined to take the high road and overlook the loss
Threatened by things outside one's control	Moved to "stand up and fight" in one's own strength	Moved to kneel down and take steps in God's power and timing
Downtrodden or defeated	Forced to take action	Drawn to "pray up" and wait on God and move in His timing, plan, and way

Ultimately, a knight uses his God-given strength for serving others, laying it all on the line, and not for self-absorption and personal enjoyment: "Blessed are you, O land whose king is of noble birth and whose princes eat at a proper time—for strength and not for drunkenness" (Ecclesiastes 10:17). In short, a knight does not use his excessive strength for creating too much personal excess. Do not get me wrong here—there are more rewards in store for those who work longer and harder at their work than for those who slack in their work, but a knight realizes that all of his resources can either be used and given away in this lifetime or be left for the survivors to divide later (which is not always a bad idea—especially if it is carefully and purposefully designated).

What is meant by strength in the context of knighthood? A knight should be strong in both spirit and body. Ultimately, a knight is victorious in battle through strength of spirit, not by flesh. The victor in a sword battle is one who fights with sheer will and spirit, not by one who competes with only mastered mechanical moves. A knight's spirit is made strong only by God by surrendering to God.

A knight's body is made strong by exercise, and, no matter what a knight's vocation or physical condition, this means exercising more than six hours per week (yes—I'm using a specific minimum because most experts agree this is, in fact, a minimum!). There are many ways to stay fit. In the knightly days of old, knights stayed fit by sports (tournaments) and hunting: "Knights must undertake such sports as to make themselves strong in prowess, yet not forget their duties."[25] This means within your own body type, strengths, and limitations working *what* you have and *however* you can for at least six hours per week. It also means eating like your body is the temple of the living God: "Do you not know that your bodies are temples of the Holy Spirit, who is in you, whom you have received from God? You are not your own; you were bought at a price. Therefore honor God with your bodies" (1 Corinthians 6:19-20).

Strength from Obedience:
The Power of a Clear Conscience

Next, I will explain one of the most effective ways possible to gain *real* strength. Strength to conquer in battle, to gain victory over personal vices, to rise up when you become weak, and to slay the "Goliaths" in your life. I am not talking about steroids or the occasional shot of adrenaline we can all muster. I am talking about real staying power— power that sustains and drives and ensues through all weakness and challenge. I am talking about the power of having a *clear conscience before God.* Consider the following biblical story about the infamous warrior Samson:

> [The Philistines] bound Samson with two new ropes and led him up from the rock. As he approached Lehi, the Philistines came toward him shouting. The Spirit of the Lord came upon him in power. The ropes on his arms became like charred flax, and the bindings dropped from his hands. So he told Delilah [his girlfriend] everything. "No razor has ever been used on my head," he said, "because I have been a Nazirite set apart to God since birth. If my head were shaved, my strength would leave me, and I would become as weak as any other man." When Delilah saw that he had told her everything, she sent word to the rulers of the Philistines, "Come back once more; he has told me everything." So the rulers of the Philistines returned with the silver in their hands. Having put him to sleep on her lap, she called a man to shave off the seven braids of his hair, and so began to subdue him. *And his strength left him.* Then she called, "Samson, the Philistines are upon you!" He awoke from his sleep and thought, "I'll go out as before and shake myself free." *But he did not know that the Lord had left him.* Then the Philistines

seized him, gouged out his eyes, and took him down to Gaza. Binding him with bronze shackles, they set him to grinding in the prison (Judges 15:13-16:21, paraphrased, emphases added).

Samson's power did not come from his hair. Obviously, God gave Samson his supernatural strength. Samson's hair only represented what gave him strength, his head represented a vow he made to God, and keeping that vow gave him the clear conscience to receive, access, and display God's power in his life. When Samson revealed the secret about his hair to Delilah, he lost his clear conscience with God and his physical and spiritual strength followed.

And now for some good news. For all of us sinners, God has a restoration plan. Notice how the story picks back up again in verse 22: "But the hair on his head began to grow again after it had been shaved." In other words, Samson's clear conscience and connection with the Lord began to grow again as he repented and obeyed. Then, after his arms were strapped to the temple pillars of the Philistines, he prayed, "O Sovereign Lord, remember me. O God, please strengthen me just once more, and let me with one blow get revenge on the Philistines for my two eyes" (v. 28), and the Lord renewed his strength in such a way that enabled him to destroy the enemy temple entirely. And in this single act, "he killed many more when he died than while he lived" (v. 30).

The New Testament also reflects this "clear conscience = power" concept. First John 3:21-22 states, "Dear friends, if our hearts do not condemn us, we have confidence before God and receive from him anything we ask, because we obey his commands and do what pleases him." As we obey, we are strengthened. And like Samson, we can fully regain our strength.

A related concept pertaining to a knight's strength is provided in Numbers 14 where Moses admonished the Israelites for moving ahead into battle without God's blessing:

When Moses reported this to all the Israelites, they mourned bitterly. Early the next morning, they went up toward the high hill country. "We have sinned," they said. "We will go up to the place the Lord promised." But Moses said, "Why are you disobeying the Lord's command? This will not succeed! Do not go up, because the Lord is not with you. You will be defeated by your enemies, for the Amalekites and Canaanites will face you there. Because you have turned away from the Lord, he will not be with you and you will fall by the sword." Nevertheless, in their presumption, they went up toward the high hill country, though neither Moses nor the ark of the Lord's covenant moved from the camp. Then the Amalekites and Canaanites who lived in that hill country came down and attacked them and beat them down all the way to Hormah (Numbers 14:39-45).

The easy-to-learn (but difficult to apply!) lesson from this story is simply do not move ahead of God or without God, for if you do, you are bound to fail.

Joshua 7:10-12 tells a similar story:

The Lord said to Joshua, "Stand up! What are you doing down on your face? Israel has sinned; they have violated my covenant, which I commanded them to keep. They have taken some of the devoted things; they have stolen, they have lied, they have put them with their own possessions. That is why the Israelites cannot stand against their enemies; they turn their backs and run because they have been made liable to destruction. I will not be with you anymore unless you destroy whatever among you is devoted to destruction."

Here we see a situation where God's presence and power was removed from His chosen people until they repented of their sin. They were unable to "stand against their enemies" until their relationship with the Lord had been restored through repentance.

By contrast, we see how God's power enabled David to become a mighty warrior because God was with him:

> Saul was afraid of David, because the Lord was with David but had left Saul. So he sent David away from him and gave him command over a thousand men, and David led the troops in their campaigns. In everything he did, he had great success, because the Lord was with him. When Saul saw how successful he was, he was afraid of him. But all Israel and Judah loved David, because he led them in their campaigns (1 Samuel 18:12-16).

Given the power and strength that comes from maintaining a clear conscience with God, to what lengths must a knight go to keep it? Consider how far Joseph went to preserve his clear conscience with God by avoiding sin:

> The Lord was with Joseph and he prospered, and he lived in the house of his Egyptian master. When his master saw that the Lord was with him and that the Lord gave him success in everything he did, Joseph found favor in his eyes and became his attendant. Potiphar put him in charge of his household, and he entrusted to his care everything he owned. From the time he put him in charge of his household and of all that he owned, the Lord blessed the household of the Egyptian because of Joseph. The blessing of

the Lord was on everything Potiphar had, both in the house and in the field. So he left in Joseph's care everything he had; with Joseph in charge, he did not concern himself with anything except the food he ate.

Now Joseph was well-built and handsome, and after a while his master's wife took notice of Joseph and said, "Come to bed with me!" But he refused. "With me in charge," he told her, "my master does not concern himself with anything in the house; everything he owns he has entrusted to my care. No one is greater in this house than I am. My master has withheld nothing from me except you, because you are his wife. How then could I do such a wicked thing and sin against God?" And though she spoke to Joseph day after day, he refused to go to bed with her or even be with her. One day he went into the house to attend to his duties, and none of the household servants was inside. She caught him by his cloak and said, "Come to bed with me!" *But he left his cloak in her hand and ran out of the house* (Genesis 39:2-12, emphasis added).

This passage shows that having a clear conscience before God and man apparently meant just about everything to Joseph.

When you survey your own strengths, you will realize that you have a few that stand out over others, as each knight has his own God-given strengths. These are yours to develop and give back to God, for you will gain more from working on your strengths than you will from trying to improve your weaknesses. Be aware of your weaknesses, but work on developing your strengths.

Do not waste your strengths or your time. Your personal comfort should be in last place relative to the cause of serving the needs of others. Ramon Lull argued that knights should even sleep on hardwood floors and not soft, fluffy beds, lest they sleep too much and lose the opportunity to serve and help others. Wow—that is quite a challenge. His point was that we should be good stewards of our time. I do not believe that Ramon Lull would recommend that modern-day knights be consumed with Facebook, online gaming, watching sports, sitcoms, etc. Indeed, there are many time stealers in our day. It is so easy to lose our time and thus our strength to these. In all things, moderation and temperance is needed.

Finally, some motivation for those hard times when your strength starts failing you, and you find yourself running out of steam: Remember that Christ gave His all for you. Every last drop of blood and sweat was left on the cross the day He died. I find this quite motivating when I find my strength missing because I missed a meal or did not get enough sleep the night before.

REFLECT

> Observe therefore all the commands I am giving you today, so that you may have the strength to go in and take over the land that you are crossing the Jordan to possess.
>
> —Deuteronomy 11:8

> David was greatly distressed because the men were talking of stoning him; each one was bitter in spirit because of his sons and daughters. But David found strength in the Lord his God.
>
> —1 Samuel 30:6

> Look to the Lord and his strength; seek his face always.
>
> —1 Chronicles 16:11

They are your servants and your people, whom you redeemed by your great strength and your mighty hand.

—Nehemiah 1:10

Do not grieve, for the joy of the Lord is your strength.

—Nehemiah 8:10

"Not by might nor by power but by my Spirit," says the Lord God Almighty.

—Zechariah 4:6

Finally, be strong in the Lord and in the strength of his might.

—Ephesians 6:10

I can do all things through him who strengthens me.

—Philippians 4:13

There is nothing as gentle as true strength, and nothing as strong as true gentleness.[26]

—Ralph Sockman

RESPOND

1. Where do we often look for strength?
2. What are some of the ways the world encourages us to build strength?
3. How are the world's sources of strength "broken cisterns"?

4. How can we practically build "real inner strength"?
5. How do we regain our strength after we lose it?
6. What is strength for? Why does God give us strength?

HUMILITY

Young men, in the same way, be submissive to those who are older. All of you, clothe yourselves with humility toward one another, because, "God opposes the proud but gives grace to the humble." Humble yourselves, therefore, under God's mighty hand, that he may lift you up in due time.

—1 Peter 5:5-6

As a prisoner for the Lord, then, I urge you to live a life worthy of the calling you have received. Be completely humble and gentle; be patient, bearing with one another in love. Make every effort to keep the unity of the Spirit through the bond of peace.

—Ephesians 4:1-3

For by the grace given me I say to every one of you: Do not think of yourself more highly than you ought, but rather think of yourself with sober judgment, in accordance with the measure of faith God has given you.

—Romans 12:3

I n God's eyes, *humility* is defined as simply putting ourselves completely under His mighty hand: "Humble yourselves in the sight of the Lord, and he shall lift you up" (James 4:10). Biblical humility can also be defined by pride, which is the perfect opposite of humility:

> God opposes the proud but gives grace to the humble (James 4:6).

> Though the Lord is on high, he looks upon the lowly, but the proud he knows from afar (Psalm 138:6).

> For whoever exalts himself will be humbled, and whoever humbles himself will be exalted (Matthew 23:12).

We are humble when we are free from pride and arrogance. And when we are humble, we are ready and available to receive God's favor and blessing. Pride, on the other hand, puts us on God's "oppose" list, and He only will know us from "afar." Being proud has a high price tag!

Sometimes we get caught up in seeking victory in every situation we encounter. We want to win in sports, in work, in life, and even in love. When we lose, disappointment comes. But what about winning and losing from God's perspective? Does he always want us to walk away with "the big win"? Consider this short lesson from the book of Joshua:

> Now when Joshua was near Jericho, he looked up and saw a man standing in front of him with a drawn sword in his hand. Joshua went up to him and asked, "Are you for us or for our enemies?" *"Neither,"* he replied, *"but as commander of the army of the Lord I have now come."* Then Joshua fell facedown to the ground in reverence, and asked him, "What message does my Lord have for his servant?" (5:13-14, emphasis added).

Here Joshua marches off to win another battle when an agent of the Lord greets him and explains that Joshua's victory is not God's priority. God's ultimate plan and victory may not be what we expect.

There may be many reasons why God does not want us to have the victory in certain situations. Keeping in mind that God always has our own good in mind (Romans 8:28), there may be several reasons why we do not win every battle. Consider these three possible reasons:

1. He wants us to learn humility and be moved to a teachable place in our lives;
2. He wants us to learn practical skills and lessons so we can win the next time we engage in a similar battle; or
3. We were not supposed to win because our reasons for doing so were either based on self-will or such a victory was not part of His ultimate plan for our lives.

Know when to retreat, as most problems and challenges that occur in a knight's life can be dealt with over time. Know when to go back and be restored.

Christ gives us the best example of true humility. Consider these two key passages of Scripture that define Christlike humility:

> Be completely humble and gentle; be patient, bearing with one another in love. Do nothing out of selfish ambition or vain conceit, but in humility consider others better than yourselves. Each of you should look not only to your own interests, but also to the interests of others. Your attitude should be the same as that of Christ Jesus: Who, being in very nature God, did not consider equality with God something to be grasped, but made himself nothing, taking the very nature of a servant, being made in human likeness. And being found in appearance as a man, he humbled himself and became obedient to death—even death on a cross! (Philippians 2:2-8).

When he had finished washing their feet, he put on his clothes and returned to his place. "Do you understand what I have done for you?" he asked them. "You call me 'Teacher' and 'Lord,' and rightly so, for that is what I am. Now that I, your Lord and Teacher, have washed your feet, you also should wash one another's feet. I have set you an example that you should do as I have done for you. I tell you the truth, no servant is greater than his master, nor is a messenger greater than the one who sent him. Now that you know these things, you will be blessed if you do them (John 13:12-17).

Notice the two extremes in the Philippians passage above: "Be *completely* humble and gentle" and "Do *nothing* out of selfish ambition or vain conceit." When friends and family are near and words are flying fast, these are difficult words to live by! Perhaps the key to living a humble life is to make humility an action in our lives rather than just an attitude. We should *be* patient, *bear with* one another, and *consider* others as better than ourselves.

REFLECT

Who is wise and understanding among you? Let him show it by his good life, by deeds done in the humility that comes from wisdom.

—James 3:13

A man's wisdom gives him patience; it is to his glory to overlook an offense.

—Proverbs 19:11

Blessed is the man who makes the Lord his trust, who does not look to the proud, to those who turn aside to false gods.

—Psalm 40:4

If a Knight is consumed with pride and seeks by that means to uphold the Order of Knighthood, he is in fact corrupting it, for his Order was founded on justice and humility with a view to protecting the humble against the proud.[27]

—Ramon Lull

RESPOND

1. Why does God oppose the proud?
2. How does being weak make us strong in God's sight?
3. Why does God give grace to the humble?
4. Why is humility a sign of true strength?
5. Is humility really lack of self-esteem?

PERSEVERANCE

> Not only so, but we also rejoice in our sufferings, because we know that
> suffering produces perseverance; perseverance, character; and character,
> hope. And hope does not disappoint us, because God has poured out his
> love into our hearts by the Holy Spirit, whom he has given us.
>
> —Romans 5:3-5

A knight needs both perseverance and patience. Perseverance is staying with a project or battle until it is finished. Patience is tolerating pain or difficulty. As stated by the Reverend Billy Graham, these two virtues are interrelated: "Patience includes perseverance—the ability to bear up under weariness, strain, and persecution when doing the work of the Lord."[28] Each of these virtues is discussed below.

PERSEVERANCE

Many medieval knights had more perseverance than we can even fathom. Imagine this: You are part of a fifteenth century army that has just traveled all day in the hot sun on horseback. You fell asleep twice on your horse during the day's travel, and you are hungry and thirsty. Your shoulders are aching, and you have a pulled muscle in your back from last week's battle. While the aching in your back is pulsating a constant, dull throb, the pain is still dwarfed by the stinging pain above your eye from a cut that has become infected. You have no medicine for the pain and swelling, nor do you have a bag of ice for your back. After arriving at camp and looking forward to a night's rest, the enemy makes a surprise attack upon your camp. Your horse is exhausted, so you take this battle on foot with whatever weapon you can scrounge.

After squaring off with your opponent, your swordplay begins, and it turns out that the opponent is an equal match to your ability. The fighting continues. Five minutes pass, and the adrenaline has already burned out of your system. Now you are down to just sheer will. Your shoulder and bicep begin to burn like they are on fire because you have been swinging a three-pound sword to save your life. The enemy keeps bringing the fight like he has rested all day for it, so the fight continues. Then you get injured as he throws an unexpected cut your way, and you feel yourself bleeding. You want to keep fighting, but now you cannot even feel your sword arm. You have no muscle left. You are panting like a dog. Your heart is pounding out of your chest. Then finally, with a lucky blow, you drop your enemy. But then you turn around, and two more are coming.

Can you imagine this situation? It is actually not too far from the truth of what many historical battles were like. Travel was hard and long. Enemies came at unsuspecting times. Many were heavily armed. Many were physically fit even beyond levels of many professional athletes today. You had to fight and persevere or lie down and die. I have engaged in swordplay while wearing armor, and it is amazing how tired you become after just ten minutes of engagement. Adrenaline can take you through the first three minutes of most battles, but then your cardiovascular system has to do all the work. And even if your arms are strong, it is only a matter of minutes before the burning sensation of muscle fatigue sets in from swinging a heavy sword over one hundred times in every direction within just a few minutes time. You cannot time your rest periods with your opponent's. When he rushes in, you need to defend—ready or not.

But life today is very similar to this in many respects. You come home from a long day at school or work, wanting only to rest, when challenges pounce into your life in moments that are sometimes perfectly timed with your moments of weakness. Perseverance is needed in these moments. To make it through these times, only true perseverance will suffice, and such perseverance is only gained through spiritual means by relying on God's promise: "I can do all things through Christ who strengthens me" (Philippians 4:13).

Perseverance takes many forms. Sometimes we need emotional perseverance—strength to get up and push through just one more day after losing a loved one. Sometimes we need spiritual perseverance to continue in prayer and seek the Lord. And sometimes we need physical perseverance. In other circumstances, we need all three. But God provides to those of us who ask—and when He gives, strength and perseverance abound.

One of the best examples of perseverance can be taken from a short mention of a warrior named Eleazar who was one of King David's three "mighty fighting men":

> Next to him was Eleazar son of Dodai the Ahohite, one of the three mighty men. He was with David at Pas Dammim when the Philistines gathered there for battle. At a place where there was a field full of barley, the troops fled from the Philistines. But they took their stand in the middle of the field. They defended it and struck the Philistines down, and the Lord brought about a great victory (1 Chronicles 11:12-14).

Second Samuel 23:9-10 fills in even more detail about this particular battle and explains that Eleazar "stood his ground and struck down the Philistines till his hand grew tired and froze to the sword." Now that's perseverance!

PATIENCE

The Bible is filled with advice regarding patience. Without patience, tact, and foresight, an ancient knight's life would go to waste. And the same goes for today's knight. Consider the following verses on patience:

> Be completely humble and gentle; be patient, bearing with one another in love (Ephesians 4:2).

> A patient man has great understanding, but a quick-tempered man displays folly (Proverbs 14:29).

> A hot-tempered man stirs up dissension, but a patient man calms a quarrel (Proverbs 15:18).

> Better a patient man than a warrior, a man who controls his temper than one who takes a city (Proverbs 16:32).

> It is not good to have zeal without knowledge, nor to be hasty and miss the way (Proverbs 19:2).

> A man's wisdom gives him patience; it is to his glory to overlook an offense (Proverbs 19:11).

> Through patience a ruler can be persuaded, and a gentle tongue can break a bone (Proverbs 25:15).

> If a ruler's anger rises against you, do not leave your post; calmness can lay great errors to rest (Ecclesiastes 10:4).

> Do not be quickly provoked in your spirit, for anger resides in the lap of fools (Ecclesiastes 7:9).

My dear brothers, take note of this: Everyone should be quick to listen, slow to speak, and slow to become angry, for man's anger does not bring about the righteous life that God desires. Therefore, get rid of all moral filth and the evil that is so prevalent and humbly accept the word planted in you, which can save you (James 1:19-21).

According to the verses above, patience (or the lack thereof) can have a powerful impact in many areas of our lives. Patience can create a situation of mutual understanding (i.e., help to build consensus), avoid foolishness and folly, turn away and disarm anger brought about by others, contain and subdue your own temper and anger, avoid dissention, calm a quarrel, help you overlook an offense, and even sway rulers and leaders.

So how do we gain this priceless virtue of patience? Patience is *grown*, not acquired. It is *slowly cultivated* in our lives, not microwaved. God can (and does) *give* us patience and wisdom as a fruit of His Spirit; God also desires to *grow* our patience by *passing us through difficult circumstances*. Consider the following Scriptures:

For our light and momentary troubles are *achieving for us* an eternal glory that far outweighs them all. So we fix our eyes not on what is seen, but on what is unseen. For what is seen is temporary, but what is unseen is eternal (2 Corinthians 4:17-18, emphasis added).

Consider it pure joy, my brothers, whenever you face trials of many kinds, because you know that the testing of your faith develops perseverance. Perseverance must finish its work so that you may be mature and complete, not lacking anything (James 1:2-4).

These passages deliver two important truths. First, God wants us to grow and mature, especially in areas of perseverance and patience. Second, He gracefully allows us to endure trials and tribulations that *build* these assets into our lives. They are often His tools to shape and refine these timeless virtues into our character. If we could actually see the incredible benefits that will come from patience that is being built in our lives by the "light and momentary troubles" (2 Corinthians 4:17), we would be truly grateful.

Blessings always seem to come after applying patience. Even if we do not receive the reward immediately, we will in the long run because we traded the stressful situation for a heap of character and wisdom that will help us through similar situations later in our lives.

REFLECT

> Then some Jews came from Antioch and Iconium and won the crowd over. They stoned Paul and dragged him outside the city, thinking he was dead. But after the disciples had gathered around him, he got up and went back into the city. The next day he and Barnabas left for Derbe.
>
> —Acts 14:19-20

> Blessed is a man who perseveres under trial; for once he has been approved, he will receive the crown of life which the Lord has promised to those who love Him.
>
> —James 1:12

> Not that I have already obtained all this, or have already been made perfect, but I press on to take hold of that for which Christ Jesus took hold of me.

Brothers, I do not consider myself yet to have taken hold of it. But one thing I do: Forgetting what is behind and straining toward what is ahead, I press on toward the goal to win the prize for which God has called me heavenward in Christ Jesus.

—Philippians 3:12-14

The reason a true knight gets up after he falls down in battle is because he knows that his life does not end on this earth.

RESPOND

1. Why is perseverance important?
2. How effective will a person's life be without perseverance?
3. How can patience shape a person's life?
4. How does suffering lead to perseverance?
5. Why does a modern-day knight need patience?
6. Think of a recent time when you lost your patience. How would the situation have turned out differently if you had remained patient? How can you stay patient better next time?

VIRTUE II

HONOR

The fear of the LORD teaches a man wisdom, and humility comes before honor.

—Proverbs 15:33

Humility and the fear of the LORD bring wealth and honor and life.

—Proverbs 22:4

Before his downfall a man's heart is proud, but humility comes before honor.

—Proverbs 18:12

Reading the three Scripture passages above leads to one clear insight: humility and honor are interrelated. Honor in the world's perspective typically deals with a person's lifestyle or accomplishments as they relate to the world's virtues. However, honor in God's eyes is very different. From God's perspective, true honor is preceded by deep humility.

What is honor? Better yet, what does it mean to be honorable in God's sight? Honor is difficult to define in a paragraph or even a lengthy story or parable. Consider these short sayings about honor that help define this complex topic:

- An honorable leader gives away all the credit but takes all the blame.
- Honor is living your life in a way that you believe God is *actually watching you.*
- Honor is giving up your bed and sleeping on the floor but saying nothing about it.
- Honor is taking the worst seat.
- Honor is being self-sacrificing and not boasting about it or complaining.
- Honor is overlooking a wrong or taking the losing position in an (ultimately unimportant) argument for the sake of peace within relationships.
- Honor is living for an audience of One.
- Honor is still finishing the details of a project even after you have been fired.
- Honor is taking the high road.
- Honor is giving a two-week notice at work and working to the best of your ability until the day you leave.
- Honor is doing your best on a school assignment even when your teacher does not deserve respect.
- Honor is looking the other way when wronged: "A man's wisdom gives him patience; it is to his glory to overlook an offense" (Proverbs 19:11).

Godly honor comes to a person when they serve and live only for God. Sometimes others acknowledge this honor publically, but this is never a true knight's goal. His first goal is to live for God and be loyal to the code of knighthood. He lives for an audience of One and thus maintains and holds honor within himself. Then whatever public honor comes, comes. Thus, a by-product of a true knight's life is likely a good reputation (at least among those where a good reputation is valued), but that's never his goal either. Nonetheless, having a good name is "more desirable than great riches; to be esteemed is better than silver or gold" (Proverbs 22:1).

The movie *Chariots of Fire* (1981) tells the true story of the British athlete, Eric Liddell, who refused to run the one-hundred-meter event in the 1924 Olympics because they were scheduled on a Sunday, which was against his spiritual convictions of working or competing on the Lord's Day, or the Sabbath. Because he refused to run in his preferred one-hundred-meter event on Sunday, they scheduled him instead to compete in the four-hundred-meter event—a much longer sprinting distance for which he had not trained. Right before the race, an American coach handed him a slip of paper with a quotation from 1 Samuel 2:30, "Those who honor me I will honor." Liddell ran the race holding the slip of paper in his hand and not only won the race but broke the existing world record with a time of 47.6 seconds. This is honor.

How do we live honorably? One way is by realizing that God is *really* watching us:

> For the eyes of the Lord range throughout the earth to strengthen those whose hearts are fully committed to him (2 Chronicles 16:9).

> The eyes of the Lord are everywhere, keeping watch on the wicked and the good (Proverbs 15:3).

And to those who seek to honor God privately and personally, God will often reward openly:

> Take heed that you do not your alms [acts of giving] before men, to be seen of them: otherwise you have no reward of your Father which is in heaven. Therefore when you do your alms, do not sound a trumpet before you, as the hypocrites do in the synagogues and in the streets, that they may have glory of men. Truly I say to you, they have their reward. But when you do alms, let not your left hand know what your right hand does: That your

alms may be in secret: and your Father which sees in secret himself shall reward you *openly*. And when you pray, you shall not be as the hypocrites are: for they love to pray standing in the synagogues and in the corners of the streets, that they may be seen of men. Truly I say to you, they have their reward. But you, when you pray, enter into your closet, and when you have shut your door, pray to your Father which is in secret; and your Father which sees in secret shall reward you *openly*. (Matthew 6:1-6 KJV, emphases added).

Honor that occurs in public is usually first earned in private by living quietly for an audience of One. Public honor often comes when you are not looking to be honored.

I heard a story about a missionary returning to America after spending years in a distant country on a mission trip. While walking off the ship, he saw the family members of other passengers rushing forward to greet their missed loved ones. Having no surviving children, he felt disappointed, as no family members came to greet him. He questioned God, "Lord, why is there no one to meet me here? I have spent my whole life serving you?" Then he heard God reply, "My child, it's because you haven't come home yet." Ultimately, our reward and honor for serving the Lord and others should come from Him and in His time.

REFLECT

He who pursues righteousness and love finds life, prosperity, and honor.

—Proverbs 21:21

A man's pride brings him low, but a man of lowly spirit gains honor.

—Proverbs 29:23

Be devoted to one another in brotherly love. Honor one another above yourselves. Never be lacking in zeal, but keep your spiritual fervor, serving the Lord. Be joyful in hope, patient in affliction, faithful in prayer.

—Romans 12:10-12

It is to a man's honor to avoid strife, but every fool is quick to quarrel.

—Proverbs 20:3

God has honored the Knight, and all the people honor him, as is recounted in this Book. And knighthood is an honorable office above all offices, orders, and estates of the world—except for the order of priesthood, which pertains to the holy sacrifice of the altar.[29]

—Ramon Lull

RESPOND

1. Is honor something we are or something we receive?
2. How should we respond when others honor us?
3. Why does the Bible connect humility and honor?
4. Why is it that whenever we seek honor we typically never receive true honor?
5. Why does humility precede true honor?

VIRTUE 12

CHARITY

Each of you should look not only to your own interests, but also to the interests of others. Your attitude should be the same as that of Christ Jesus: Who, being in very nature God, did not consider equality with God something to be grasped, but made himself nothing, taking the very nature of a servant, being made in human likeness.

—Philippians 2:4-7

Nobody should seek his own good, but the good of others.

—1 Corinthians 10:24

The word used to translate the Greek word *agape* in most modern English Bibles is *love*, but in many older translations, *agape* was translated as "charity" when it was used in a context of one person to another. In this way, charity was defined as unlimited loving-kindness toward all others. In a biblical context, this term should not be mistaken for the more modern use of the word to mean only giving to those in need (i.e., "giving to charity"), although this can be a substantial part of what's meant by the word. A more encompassing definition of the word *charity*, at least in the context of a modern-day knight, would be to be charitable (or giving) to others with his or her time, talent, and treasures. Let's review each.

A knight's time and talents are not his or her own, as they belong to the body of Christ, but they are his to *manage*. See the difference? If you are involved in a ministry or giving effort that's not in line with your natural and God-given gifts and talents, maybe it is time to change ministries. If your time is, however, well suited for the endeavor, stay involved and give your time and talent with purpose, vigor, and intention. To those knights who are not directly involved in the ministry world, tithe your time (by giving ten percent or more) to a ministry that aligns with your gifts and talents. And about your time specifically, if too much of your time is being consumed by service so that your top game is not being offered, govern your time by retreating and resting until it is. Sometimes the most godly thing you can do is take a nap, which Christ did regularly even during the peak of his ministry seasons.

A knight's treasure is not his or her own, but it is his or hers to both *grow* and *give away* at the *right time* and in the *right way*—for a true knight *earns all they can, saves all they can, and gives away all they can.* To a true knight, money is only a resource. It is a tool to accomplish good and to fuel the working hand of God in his community, cause, and purpose in life. Even saving money until the end of your life is okay, provided that you have set up a way to give it all away with intention and purpose upon death: "A good man leaves an inheritance for his children's children, but a sinner's wealth is stored up for the righteous" (Proverbs 13:22).

A true knight is generous and realizes that all wealth will eventually and intentionally be used for God's kingdom: "Though your riches increase, do not set your heart on them" (Psalm 62:10b; see also Luke 12:21, where Jesus' parable conveys that those who have wealth should be "rich towards God"). The knight who works diligently in life will be granted the gift to enjoy the fruit of his labor: "Then I realized that it is good and proper for a man to eat and drink, and to find satisfaction in his toilsome labor under the sun during the few days of life God has given him—for this is his lot. Moreover, when God gives any man wealth and possessions, and enables him to enjoy them, to accept his lot and be happy in his work—this is a gift of God. He seldom reflects on the days of his life, because God keeps him occupied with gladness of heart" (Ecclesiastes 5:18-20).

There is nothing wrong with enjoying the fruit of your labor, within reason (see Deuteronomy 14). Just be assured that only in God does life have meaning and true pleasure. Without Him, nothing satisfies, but with Him, we find satisfaction and enjoyment. True pleasure comes only when we acknowledge and revere God (Deuteronomy 12:13). Riches do not satisfy, but Christ does (see John 7:37-38).

So how can a knight intentionally and effectively give to help the needs of the poor? First, it is important to understand that we are commanded to do so:

> He who is kind to the poor lends to the Lord, and he will reward him for what he has done (Proverbs 19:17).

> If a man shuts his ears to the cry of the poor, he too will cry out and not be answered (Proverbs 21:13).

God cares deeply about the poor. There are hundreds of verses in the Bible about the poor and God's heart for them. The two verses above show how God's promises are specific to our lives and are intertwined with our choices, including how we respond to the poor He places in our life circle. Consider Christ's expressions of love for the poor:

> Then the righteous will answer him, "Lord, when did we see you hungry and feed you, or thirsty and give you something to drink? When did we see you a stranger and invite you in, or needing clothes and clothe you? When did we see you sick or in prison and go to visit you?" The King will reply, "I tell you the truth, whatever you did for one of the least of

these brothers of mine, you did for me" (Matthew 25:37-40).

By loving the poor, we love God. Mother Teresa once said, "Only in heaven will we see how much we owe to the poor for helping us to love God better because of them." But we also need to be careful in deciding if we should give and how we should give. Sometimes giving money to those in need can hinder more than it can help because giving money to people who refuse to change their irresponsible spending habits can be a huge mistake (now they'll just be spending *your* money unwisely!). Working with your church's benevolence group or consulting other resources can help you answer the "if" question about giving. Some biblically sound benevolence guidelines are published by Crown Financial Ministries and can be found online at http://www.crown.org.

· When it comes to giving (especially financial giving), many are quick to put up defenses: "The poor are poor because of their own bad choices. Why don't they just pull themselves together, start working for a living, go from one good job to a better job and build a successful life like I did? If this is how I did it in life, why should it be any different for them?"

This line of thinking carelessly stereotypes needy individuals. While these assumptions may be true about some, they are not true about many of the people who are currently in need. You really have no idea how they arrived at their place in life. Whether or not we would like to admit this, there is even a chance we would have been worse off if we had lived their lives! Let's imagine these assumptions are completely true about the particular poor that God has placed in your life. Does this mean we should not have mercy and grace on them? We must be mindful of the Proverb: "If a man shuts his ears to the cry of the poor, he too will cry out and not be answered" (21:13).

We can apply these truths to our lives by considering every encounter with others as divine appointments: "For we are God's workmanship, created in Christ Jesus to do good works, which God prepared in advance for us to do" (Ephesians 2:10). Where will your feet take you? How will you respond the next time God brings you the poor, in whatever form they come? When the Lord scribed Proverbs 19:17 through Solomon ("He who is kind to the poor lends to the Lord, and he will reward him for what he has done"), He was making a very straightforward proposal, "You help the poor, and I will repay you."

REFLECT

Religion that God our Father accepts as pure and faultless is this: to look after orphans and widows in their distress and to keep oneself from being polluted by the world.

—James 1:27

Let us touch the dying, the poor, the lonely, and the unwanted according to the graces we have received and let us not be ashamed or slow to do the humble work.[30]

—Mother Teresa

For what purpose do you desire to enter the Order? If it be riches, to take your ease, and be held in honor without doing honor to Knighthood, you are unworthy of it.[31]

—Will Durant

RESPOND

1. How does God show us when and how much to give?
2. In what circumstances can giving actually hurt someone?

3. What are some practical ways you can earn all you can, save all you can, and give away all you can?
4. What are some ways we can be charitable to others that don't require money?
5. When has someone's charitable actions positively impacted your life?

SACRIFICE

> Then Jesus said to his disciples, "If anyone would come after me, he must deny himself and take up his cross and follow me. For whoever wants to save his life will lose it, but whoever loses his life for me will find it." What good will it be for a man if he gains the whole world, yet forfeits his soul? Or what can a man give in exchange for his soul?
>
> —Matthew 16:24-25

Common definitions of *sacrifice* will both underestimate and poorly define the concept, at least when the term is considered from a biblical perspective. Let's start with a common definition from dictionaries. *Sacrifice* means "The offering of animal, plant, or human life or of some material possession to a deity, as in propitiation or homage."[32] Defining sacrifice in the Christian sense of the word requires a more complicated description. Let's take a look at the five principles of sacrifice provided by Ed Rickard.[33]

PRINCIPLE 1: SOME SACRIFICE IS NO SACRIFICE

In Malachi 1:7-8, God explains to the priests that He is less than pleased with their halfhearted sacrifice:

> You place defiled food on my altar. But you ask, "How have we defiled you?" By saying that the Lord's table is contemptible. When you bring blind animals for sacrifice, is that not wrong? When you sacrifice crippled or diseased animals, is that not wrong? Try offering them to your governor! Would he be pleased with you? Would he accept you? says the Lord Almighty.

How many times do we offer our best to our employers but leave the leftovers for God? Surely we should give our best in both arenas.

PRINCIPLE 2: GOD WANTS ONLY ONE THING, AND THAT IS EVERYTHING

Psalm 50:10 reminds us that God owns it all in the first place: "For every animal of the forest is mine, and the cattle on a thousand hills." God obviously knows that He owns it all, but what He wants from us is to acknowledge this fact and give it all back to Him. When Jesus said, "If anyone comes to me and does not hate his father and mother, his wife and children, his brothers and sisters—yes, even his own life—he cannot be my disciple," (Luke 14:26) He was simply saying that we need to value and prioritize our relationship with Christ *over all others*. He continues in this same passage by saying, "And anyone who does not carry his cross and follow me cannot be my disciple" (v. 27). Then He tells a story that illustrates if you are going to do anything significant with impact, you need to be "all in":

> Suppose one of you wants to build a tower. Will he not first sit down and estimate the cost to see if he has enough money to complete it? For if he lays the foundation and is not able to finish it, everyone who sees it will ridicule him, saying, "This fellow began to build and was not able to finish." Or suppose a

king is about to go to war against another king. Will
he not first sit down and consider whether he is able
with ten thousand men to oppose the one coming
against him with twenty thousand? If he is not able,
he will send a delegation while the other is still a long
way off and will ask for terms of peace. In the same
way, any of you who does not give up everything he
has cannot be my disciple (Luke 14:28-33).

PRINCIPLE 3: THERE IS NO SUCH THING AS SACRIFICE

While God entrusts us with resources, gifts, and talents while we are
here on Earth, we really do not own anything in the first place and
have to turn it all in when we die. I remember painting my mom's
house when I was a teenager and learning this fact in the most
simplistic way. While I was painting her house, I felt like I was doing
a noble act for her by sacrificing my time to do so. Then, while I was
watching my hands and wrist flex with every brushstroke, it suddenly
dawned on me that I could not even make this simple movement if
God did not equip me to do so. What then was mine to sacrifice in
the first place?

PRINCIPLE 4: IT IS NOT POSSIBLE TO AVOID SACRIFICE

Guess what? You are going to make a sacrifice someday—in fact, you
are going to sacrifice it *all*. We get to play the game while on this
earth, but the day comes for each of us when we get to "turn in all
of the chips." It is better to be a willing participant in the sacrificing
process than a surprised one who played the game believing the chips
belonged to them.

PRINCIPLE 5: SACRIFICE IS THE KEY TO BLESSING

This final principle is the good news about sacrifice: If we give it all
up, we gain what was not even ours in the first place and so much

more. This principle holds true when it comes to the most important thing—eternal life—as well as our lives here on Earth: "He is no fool who gives what he cannot keep to gain what he cannot lose."[34] Consider these promises from Scripture that are given to those who sacrifice all and dedicate all to the Lord:

> For the eyes of the Lord range throughout the earth to strengthen those whose hearts are fully committed to him (2 Chronicles 16:9).

> And everyone who has left houses or brothers or sisters or father or mother or children or fields for my sake will receive a hundred times as much and will inherit eternal life (Matthew 19:29).

> But seek first his kingdom and his righteousness, and all these things will be given to you as well (Matthew 6:33).

> "I tell you the truth," Jesus replied, "no one who has left home or brothers or sisters or mother or father or children or fields for me will fail to receive a hundred times as much in this present age (homes, brothers, sisters, mothers, children, and fields—and with them, persecutions) and in the age to come, eternal life. But many who are first will be last, and the last first" (Mark 10:29-31).

Christ *voluntarily* emptied Himself of anything and everything that stood in the way of the glory and gain of His Father through Him. Our response is to sacrifice our pleasures, rights, privileges, possessions, expectations, and even our plans to the Lord. Next, let's turn to an example of complete sacrifice made by a knight of old—a famous knight named Roland.

It was Saturday evening, August 15, 778 AD. On this hot summer night, French Prince Charlemagne marched his army through the dangerous Roncevaux Mountain Pass in the Pyrenees, completely unaware that he was leading his troops straight into an ambush. A large guerilla force of Basques (who were very familiar with the terrain) attacked Charlemagne's rearguard and began decimating the army, plundering their baggage wagons and stealing their gold.

Sizing up the situation and the odds, three of Charlemagne's most valiant knights, Egginhard (who was mayor of the palace), Anselmus (a high-ranking count), and Roland left their stations in the march and headed straight back to the rearguard to join the fight. Their goal was not to win the battle—for they knew they were far too outnumbered to pull off a victory that day. They fought knowing that the very best they could do was hassle the enemy for as long as possible to allow the others to escape. All three men died that day, but they saved thousands.

A knight's most honorable service is one of sacrifice—sacrifice of his or her time, talents, and treasure for the kingdom's sake and for others. The ultimate sacrifice was laid down by Christ, who gave His life for us. And even Christ recognized that the sacrifice of one's life is the greatest expression of love: "Greater love has no one than this, that he lay down his life for his friends" (John 15:13).

While the greatest sacrifice may indeed be laying down our lives for others, there is a way to do this while still living to fight another day. The book of Isaiah provides a great contrast between fasting *our* way versus *God's* way. In fact, this passage explains that one of the best ways we can fast (and sacrifice) our life to God and for the benefit of others is by how we *live*:

OUR WAY OF FASTING

> "Why have we fasted," they say, "and you have not seen it? Why have we humbled ourselves, and you have not noticed?" Yet on the day of your fasting, you do as you please and exploit all your workers.

> Your fasting ends in quarreling and strife and in
> striking each other with wicked fists. You cannot
> fast as you do today and expect your voice to be
> heard on high. Is this the kind of fast I have chosen,
> only a day for a man to humble himself? Is it only
> for bowing one's head like a reed and for lying on
> sackcloth and ashes? Is that what you call a fast, a
> day acceptable to the Lord? (Isaiah 58:3-5).

The above passage shows how God is displeased with sacrifice when we are doing it for the wrong reasons or when our hearts are not in it. We should not believe that we can fool God and earn spiritual points by making only physical sacrifices. True sacrifice requires the heart, lest we lose both the opportunity to make a genuine sacrifice as well as the blessing we would have received had our hearts been in it the first time. Now compare the above type of fasting with:

GOD'S WAY OF FASTING

> Is not this the kind of fasting I have chosen: to loose
> the chains of injustice and untie the cords of the
> yoke, to set the oppressed free and break every yoke?
> Is it not to share your food with the hungry and to
> provide the poor wanderer with shelter—when you
> see the naked, to clothe him, and not to turn away
> from your own flesh and blood? Then your light
> will break forth like the dawn, and your healing
> will quickly appear; then your righteousness will go
> before you, and the glory of the Lord will be your
> rearguard. Then you will call, and the Lord will
> answer; you will cry for help, and he will say: "Here
> am I." If you do away with the yoke of oppression,
> with the pointing finger and malicious talk, and if
> you spend yourselves in behalf of the hungry and
> satisfy the needs of the oppressed, then your light

will rise in the darkness, and your night will become like the noonday. The Lord will guide you always; he will satisfy your needs in a sun-scorched land and will strengthen your frame. You will be like a well-watered garden, like a spring whose waters never fail. Your people will rebuild the ancient ruins and will raise up the age-old foundations; you will be called Repairer of Broken Walls, Restorer of Streets with Dwellings (Isaiah 58:6-12).

This passage shows that a knight's way of sacrifice is by *using his strength on behalf of the weak.* Loosing the chains of injustice, untying the cords of bondage, setting the oppressed free—these are all feats of strength that are used on behalf of the needy. And sharing our food and providing the wanderer with shelter and clothing are acts of sacrifice. We are to spend ourselves on behalf of the hungry and satisfy the needs of the oppressed—that is true sacrifice. Then God's blessing pours into our lives—breaking forth like the dawn, with the glory of the Lord as our rearguard, and our nights become like the noonday. God's guidance will be with us always, and he will strengthen our frame.

A final thought about sacrifice: Do not whine, complain, or boast about your sacrifice. The Lord sees your sacrifice, and He will reward you openly before men for what you have done in private (Matthew 6:1-6).

REFLECT

I tell you the truth, unless a kernel of wheat falls to the ground and dies, it remains only a single seed. But if it dies, it produces many seeds. The man who loves his life will lose it, while the man who hates his life in this world will keep it for eternal life. Whoever serves me must follow me; and where I

am, my servant also will be. My Father will honor
the one who serves me.

—John 12:24-26

I only know that in every city the Holy Spirit
warns me that prison and hardships are facing me.
However, I consider my life worth nothing to me,
if only I may finish the race and complete the task
the Lord Jesus has given me—the task of testifying
to the gospel of God's grace.

—Acts 20:23-24

Still another said to Jesus, "I will follow you, Lord;
but first let me go back and say good-bye to my
family." Jesus replied, "No one who puts his hand
to the plow and looks back is fit for service in the
kingdom of God."

—Luke 9:61-62

RESPOND

1. How might God test us with making small sacrifices before
   He asks us to make larger ones?
2. How does making sacrifices show our faith and trust in God?
3. What are some of the circumstances where we should not
   make sacrifices, even if they might seem like good sacrifices
   to others?
4. How can we be sure that our heart is in the sacrifices we make?
5. If we sacrifice our strength on behalf of others, how can we
   be sure to fill ourselves back up again to be ready for new
   opportunities to serve?

COMPASSION

Speak up for those who cannot speak for themselves, for the rights of all who are destitute. Speak up and judge fairly; defend the rights of the poor and needy.

—Proverbs 31:8-9

Be kind and compassionate to one another, forgiving each other, just as in Christ God forgave you.

—Ephesians 4:32

Having compassion simply means to possess a deep feeling of sympathy and sorrow for those who are stricken by misfortune, coupled with a strong desire to alleviate their suffering. Ramon Lull explains that one of a knight's key roles is to perform acts of compassion:

> The Knight must maintain and defend women and respect and defend those less powerful than he. The office of a knight is to maintain and defend women, widows and orphans, men diseased; and those who are neither powerful nor strong. For as custom and reason is that the greatest and most mighty helps

the feeble and the lesser, and that they should have recourse to the great.[35]

The Civil War was a controversial war with devout and authentic Christians who fought on both sides—the North and the South. One of the generals from the South, Robert E. Lee, demonstrated compassion in a powerful way when he encountered an injured soldier from the North. The soldier himself recounted the following story:

> I was at the battle of Gettysburg myself, and an incident occurred there which largely changed my views of the Southern people. I had been a most bitter anti-South man and fought and cursed the Confederates desperately. I could see nothing good in any of them. The last day of the fight, I was badly wounded. A ball shattered my left leg. I lay on the ground not far from Cemetery Ridge, and as General Lee ordered his retreat, he and his officers rode near me. As he came along, I recognized him, and though faint from exposure and loss of blood, I raised up my hands, looked Lee in the face, and shouted as loud as I could, "Hurrah for the Union!" The general heard me, looked, stopped his horse, dismounted, and came toward me. I confess that I at first thought he meant to kill me. But as he came up, he looked down at me with such a sad expression upon his face that all fear left me, and I wondered what he was about. He extended his hand to me and grasping mine firmly and looking right into my eyes, said, "My son, I hope you will soon be well."
>
> If I live a thousand years I shall never forget the expression on General Lee's face. There he was, defeated, retiring from a field that had cost him and

his cause almost their last hope, and yet he stopped to say words like those to a wounded soldier of the opposition who had taunted him as he passed by! As soon as the general had left me, I cried myself to sleep there upon the bloody ground.[36]

This is an incredible example of compassion. Finding this enemy soldier in the middle of a war, General Lee could have done anything—he could have passed by, he could have insulted him in return, he could have even killed him. But instead, he showed the soldier mercy and compassion.

Next, let's take a look at displays of compassion made by Christ:

> When he saw the crowds, he had compassion on them, because they were harassed and helpless, like sheep without a shepherd (Matthew 9:36).

> When Jesus heard what had happened, he withdrew by boat privately to a solitary place. Hearing of this, the crowds followed him on foot from the towns. When Jesus landed and saw a large crowd, he had compassion on them and healed their sick (Matthew 14:13-14).

> Great crowds came to him, bringing the lame, the blind, the crippled, the mute, and many others and laid them at his feet; and he healed them. The people were amazed when they saw the mute speaking, the crippled made well, the lame walking, and the blind seeing. And they praised the God of Israel. Jesus called his disciples to him and said, "I have compassion for these people; they have already been with me three days and have nothing to eat. I do

not want to send them away hungry, or they may collapse on the way'" (Matthew 15:30-32).

Two blind men were sitting by the roadside, and when they heard that Jesus was going by, they shouted, "Lord, Son of David, have mercy on us!" The crowd rebuked them and told them to be quiet, but they shouted all the louder, "Lord, Son of David, have mercy on us!" Jesus stopped and called them. "What do you want me to do for you?" he asked. "Lord," they answered, "we want our sight." Jesus had compassion on them and touched their eyes. Immediately they received their sight and followed him. (Matthew 20:30-34).

A man with leprosy came to him and begged him on his knees, "If you are willing, you can make me clean." Filled with compassion, Jesus reached out his hand and touched the man. "I am willing," he said. "Be clean!" Immediately the leprosy left him and he was cured (Mark 1:40-42).

Jesus did not have much of a filter for choosing who to help—when He was led to have compassion on those around them, He gave whatever He had based on whatever they needed. When He saw a need, he met it. Biblical giving is radical at times but should be balanced based on different circumstances (see the Virtue 12: Charity).

Compassion is when you stop your busy life to pour into the needs of others. It is an active requirement of any modern knight's daily life.

REFLECT

Knights who have eyes which cannot see the feeble and weak, have not the heart nor the might by which they may record the deeds to be in the Order of Knighthood.

—Ramon Lull

Praise be to the God and Father of our Lord Jesus Christ, the Father of compassion and the God of all comfort, who comforts us in all our troubles, so that we can comfort those in any trouble with the comfort we ourselves have received from God. For just as the sufferings of Christ flow over into our lives, so also through Christ our comfort overflows.

—2 Corinthians 1:3-5

As you know, we consider blessed those who have persevered. You have heard of Job's perseverance and have seen what the Lord finally brought about. The Lord is full of compassion and mercy.

—James 5:11

RESPOND

1. How will you know when to have compassion on someone, and how you should act (see Ephesians 2:8-10)?
2. How should acts of compassion made by Christians differ from others' acts of compassion (see Luke 6:27-36)?
3. Is it ever appropriate not to show compassion?
4. How did Christ have compassion on others?
5. How can we show compassion to others in ways that do not require money?]

LOYALTY

> If anyone comes to me and does not hate his father and mother, his wife and children, his brothers and sisters—yes, even his own life—he cannot be my disciple. And anyone who does not carry his cross and follow me cannot be my disciple.
>
> —Luke 14:26-27

Perhaps the clearest way to define loyalty is: *unswerving in allegiance*. We are all on different paths in life; when you choose to not swerve from the path the Lord has for you, that's loyalty. When you have the opportunity to veer from the path of friendship or marriage but choose not to, you are acting out of loyalty. Loyalty can also be explained as faithful dedication.

Reverend John Newton provides a broader definition of loyalty. Drawing from the book, *Married for Good*,[37] he describes four kinds of loyalty that we ought to consider in any type of relationship:

- First, there is *attitudinal* loyalty, which seeks to see the other person from Christ's perspective, concentrating on their qualities rather than their faults.

- Secondly, there is *verbal* loyalty, choosing both how we address other people and how we speak about them when they are not around.
- Thirdly, there is *spiritual* loyalty, which very often amounts to nothing more complicated than respect, releasing people to be themselves rather than having our own agendas for them, loving them for who they are rather than for what we think they might become.
- And fourthly, there is *heart* loyalty, a commitment to stay in relationship with another person no matter what—a willingness to work together on difficulties and to work out differences together.[38]

Loyalty in all four of these areas is needed in one's life. It is difficult to understand the importance and significance of loyalty until you have been betrayed in any of these areas. I have been betrayed a few times in life by people I trusted. Betraying a trust or a relationship can cause chasms between people that last for years, even a lifetime. It was only after going through the process that I began to understand just how important loyalty is with the relationship I have with the Lord.

Fortunately, we have a Master who understands betrayal like no other. Christ was betrayed by Judas in a way that led to His death. He was even betrayed during his final trial by his best friend, Peter.

Loyalty was one of the key traits of knighthood. Young pages were turned into squires and then knights, all under the king, prince, or baron's castle. The king fed, housed, and trained the knight for years (sometimes beginning at age eight as a young page), so it was a clear expectation of the young knight to use those same skills and fortitude in service for the king.

Because training was costly, kings wanted to make sure that their investment was one that would pay off. If they invested years of training into a knight only to have them run off to another kingdom, their entire investment was lost. As a knight for Christ, should we be any different? If the Lord Jesus Himself lived and died for us, shouldn't we commit and give our *all* to Him? He deserves our loyalty in every way, our actions, our words, even our thoughts.

Pay close attention to this next part because it is important. Do you know that God Himself gives preferential treatment to those who demonstrate loyalty through obedience to Him by living an upright and pure life? Yes, God has special servants; knights whom He appoints listen to His prompting and do His bidding. From Mother Teresa and Billy Graham to everyday believers, God has a *special relationship* with those who follow Him daily by locking onto the path of purity. Do you find this hard to believe? Consider Proverbs 3:32: "For the Lord detests a perverse man but takes the upright into his confidence."

What an invitation! How would you like to gain the confidence and trust of the One who created the entire universe? The One who framed the first man and gave him His first breath? Does this sound like an honor? Perhaps honor is an understatement! Likewise, how can the God of the entire universe take a fallen, sinful person *into His confidence*? Consider these similar promises from God's word:

> If a man cleanses himself from the latter [wickedness and godless living], he will be an instrument for noble purposes, made holy, useful to the Master and prepared to do any good work (2 Timothy 2:21).

> The Lord confides in those who fear him; he makes his covenant known to them (Psalm 25:14).

> I no longer call you servants, because a servant does not know his master's business. Instead, I have called you friends, for everything that I learned from my Father I have made known to you. You did not choose me, but I chose you and appointed you to go and bear fruit—fruit that will last. Then the Father

will give you whatever you ask in my name. This is my command: Love each other (John 15:15-17).

Have no misunderstanding—being an upright person does not mean being perfect; it means being upright. In fact, the original language for this term contains the idea of "being straight" and "not twisted or bent." When professional ice skaters perform, their goal is to *stay upright* until their performance ends. If they fall, they get right back up. Proverbs 24:16 declares the same goal for our lives: "Though a righteous man falls seven times, he rises again, but the wicked are brought down by calamity." And loyal knights get back on the horse after falling down.

Biblical history gives us many real-life examples of people who were not perfect but were still upright. David was referred to as "a man after God's own heart" in 1 Samuel 13:14, yet David fell into an affair. But God still took David into His confidence. Jeremiah was depressed, Jonah ran away from God, Paul murdered, Martha worried too much, and Elijah burned out. All these people fell, but through their loyalty to the Lord and their faith, they came back upright until their performance, their lives, ended. God used them and brought them into His confidence.

Finally, consider these examples of how fighting men—knights of old—demonstrated loyalty to God and their earthly king (David), even when others deserted:

> Men of Zebulun [were] experienced soldiers prepared for battle with every type of weapon, to help David with *undivided loyalty*—50,000" (1 Chronicles 12:33, emphasis added).

> Next to him was Eleazar son of Dodai the Ahohite. As one of the three mighty men, he was with David when they taunted the Philistines gathered at Pas Dammim for battle. *Then the men of Israel retreated, but he stood his ground and struck down the Philistines*

till his hand grew tired and froze to the sword. The Lord brought about a great victory that day. The troops returned to Eleazar, but only to strip the dead (2 Samuel 23:9-10, emphasis added).

Next to him was Shammah son of Agee the Hararite. When the Philistines banded together at a place where there was a field full of lentils, *Israel's troops fled from them. But Shammah took his stand in the middle of the field.* He defended it and struck the Philistines down, and the Lord brought about a great victory (2 Samuel 23:11-12, emphasis added).

David's fighting men were so loyal to him that they even risked their lives to bring him a cup of water from behind enemy lines:

During harvest time, three of the thirty chief men came down to David at the cave of Adullam, while a band of Philistines was encamped in the Valley of Rephaim. At that time, David was in the stronghold, and the Philistine garrison was at Bethlehem. David longed for water and said, "Oh, that someone would get me a drink of water from the well near the gate of Bethlehem!" So the three mighty men broke through the Philistine lines, drew water from the well near the gate of Bethlehem, and carried it back to David. But he refused to drink it; instead, he poured it out before the Lord. "Far be it from me, O Lord, to do this!" he said. "Is it not the blood of men who went at the risk of their lives?" And David would not drink it (2 Samuel 23:13-17).

Among all these examples, however, we see no greater example than Christ, who when faced with a painful death met the challenge with: "Father, if thou be willing, remove this cup from me: nevertheless not my will, but thine, be done" (Luke 22:42).

REFLECT

> When charity, loyalty, integrity, justice, and truth grew weak in the world, then there began cruelty, injury, disloyalty and falseness. Thus error and trouble came into the very world where God had planned for man to know, love, serve, fear, and honor Him. Fortunately, however, no sooner had laxness in enforcing the law first arisen than fear in turn caused justice to be restored to the honor in which she was formerly held. Therefore, all the people were divided by thousands. Out of each thousand, there was chosen a man more notable than all the rest for his loyalty, his strength, his noble courage, his breeding and his manners.[39]

—Ramon Lull

RESPOND

1. When do you find it the most difficult to be loyal to your relationship with Christ? With friends? With family?
2. Describe a recent occasion where you had the opportunity to be disloyal but chose to be loyal.
3. How has someone's disloyalty impacted your life?
4. How does one become more loyal?
5. Christ was loyal to the death out of obedience to His Father. How does this encourage you to be loyal in the daily choices of your life?

TRUTH

> I have chosen the way of truth; I have set my heart on your laws. I hold fast to your statutes, O LORD. Do not let me be put to shame. I run in the path of your commands, for you have set my heart free.
>
> —Psalm 119:30-32
>
> Test me, O LORD, and try me, examine my heart and my mind; for your love is ever before me, and I walk continually in your truth. I do not sit with deceitful men, nor do I consort with hypocrites; I abhor the assembly of evildoers and refuse to sit with the wicked. I wash my hands in innocence, and go about your altar, O LORD.
>
> —Psalm 26:2-6

Being truthful means being real and honest with the facts, but it also means living in a way where what you know to be true influences your daily actions. A knight who has not yet fully resolved that he will speak only the truth will stumble. Somewhere, sometime, somehow, part of his life will crumble without holding to the virtue of truth. Consider the following Scriptures:

A truthful witness gives honest testimony, but a false witness tells lies (Proverbs 12:17).

The Lord detests lying lips, but he delights in men who are truthful (Proverbs 12:22).

A truthful witness does not deceive, but a false witness pours out lies (Proverbs 14:5).

A truthful witness saves lives, but a false witness is deceitful (Proverbs 14:25).

When describing spiritual armor, the apostle Paul uses the warrior's belt to signify truth: "Stand firm then, with the belt of truth buckled around your waist" (Ephesians 6:14). Think about the significance of the belt as part of a knight's armor. If you are in the middle of a sword battle and your belt falls down, three things can happen: (1) you lose your backup weapons (most knights strapped daggers to their weapon belt); (2) you lose focus as your clothing flies to the wind; and (3) you cannot move as fast and be as agile as you could be if your belt and clothing are secure. Just like in real life, if we stop telling the truth, we do not have a clear conscience to use all of our battle weapons, we become distracted as we get tangled in a massive web of lies, and we cannot move forth with clarity of mind and purpose.

Being truthful also includes being sincere and candid with friends and loved ones. A true knight values truth over friendship; he will tell a friend when he is in trouble or going astray, having more concern for the long-term wellbeing of his friend than the short-term friendship. At times, we must be ready to wound a friend and risk a friendship by confronting someone when we are convinced it is our time to act. In doing this, we may suffer short-term discontent in exchange for long-term favor from the person later (Proverbs 28:23). Biblical confrontation should be done gently, with sincerity and without hypocrisy. Consider these guidelines:

Brothers, if someone is caught in a sin, you who are spiritual should restore him gently. But watch yourself, or you also may be tempted. Carry each other's burdens, and in this way you will fulfill the law of Christ (Galatians 6:1-2).

Why do you look at the speck of sawdust in your brother's eye and pay no attention to the plank in your own eye? How can you say to your brother, "Let me take the speck out of your eye," when all the time there is a plank in your own eye? You hypocrite, first take the plank out of your own eye, and then you will see clearly to remove the speck from your brother's eye (Matthew 7:3-5).

To truly express Christ's love, we must be sincere. In fact, the apostle Paul says that sincerity and true love must go hand in hand. "Love must be sincere. Hate what is evil; cling to what is good" (Romans 10:9). Yes, certainly it helps to be tactful, but we need to pull the trigger when God puts the target opportunity before us. Consider the passage below regarding Ezekiel being a watchman for God:

The word of the Lord came to me: "Son of man, speak to your countrymen and say to them: 'When I bring the sword against a land, and the people of the land choose one of their men and make him their watchman, and he sees the sword coming against the land and blows the trumpet to warn the people, then if anyone hears the trumpet but does not take warning and the sword comes and takes his life, his blood will be on his own head. Since he heard the sound of the trumpet but did not take warning, his blood will be on his own head. If he had taken warning, he would have saved himself. But if the watchman sees the sword coming and does not blow the trumpet to warn the people and the sword comes and takes the life of one of them, that man will be taken away because of his sin, but I will hold the watchman accountable for his blood.' Son of man, I have made you a watchman for the house of Israel; so hear the word I speak and give them warning from me. When I say to the wicked, 'O wicked man, you will surely die,' and you do not speak out to dissuade him from his ways, that wicked man will die for his sin, and I will hold you accountable for his blood. But if you do warn the wicked man to turn from his ways and he does not do so, he will die for his sin, but you will have saved yourself" (Ezekiel 33:1-9).

This story sums up the principle well. If it is your time and your job to be honest with someone about an issue for their own long-term good or for the good of others and you do not do it, you may be held accountable by God. That is quite a burden to bear. The easy way out of these difficult situations is to confront them tactfully with the truth. Ultimately, you should let your concern regarding your own accountability to God govern your actions more than your fear of the person's negative response.

REFLECT

"At all times speak the truth."

—Charlemagne's Code of Chivalry

Always tell the truth; that way you will never have to remember what you've said.

RESPOND

1. When have you had the opportunity to confront someone about an issue but chose not to? What was the outcome?

2. How can we share the truth *in love* with someone?
3. When are "white lies" okay to tell?
4. How has someone's lack of truthfulness hurt you in the past?
5. Why are we still tempted to lie when we know that God sees our hearts?

VIRTUE 17

PURITY

LORD, who may dwell in your sanctuary? Who may live on your holy hill? He whose walk is blameless and who does what is righteous, who speaks the truth from his heart and has no slander on his tongue, who does his neighbor no wrong and casts no slur on his fellowman, who despises a vile man but honors those who fear the LORD, who keeps his oath even when it hurts, who lends his money without usury and does not accept a bribe against the innocent. He who does these things will never be shaken.

—Psalm 15

But among you there must not be even a hint of sexual immorality, or of any kind of impurity, or of greed, because these are improper for God's holy people. Nor should there be obscenity, foolish talk, or coarse joking, which are out of place, but rather thanksgiving. For of this you can be sure: No immoral, impure, or greedy person—such a man is an idolater—has any inheritance in the kingdom of Christ and of God.

—Ephesians 5:3-5

Webster's definition of *purity* is, "Free from anything that taints, impairs; clear, unmixed."[40] Applying this concept to a Christian's life is not much different—God wants us to be free from life-impairing sin (Hebrews 12:1) that grieves the Holy Spirit (Ephesians 4:30). He also wants us to be pure in the sense that we are unmixed with the things of this world (2 Timothy 2:4-6; Galatians 6:14).

How is such purity achieved? Let's break the process into two steps. First, we are made *positionally pure* before God when we receive Christ. When we receive Christ, we transition from children under God's judgment and wrath to adopted, forgiven children (Romans 5:9-11; John 3:16-36). Then, we go through a lifelong process of *progressive purification* (2 Corinthians 7:1; 1 John 3:3-6; James 2). The first purification is a gift that we receive by faith. The second is a process that takes a lifetime, and one that is never finalized until after we die. The Lord works on us continually (as we submit to Him), as He is the author and finisher of our faith (Philippians 1:6).

Before we take a look at the areas of our lives that He desires to purify, let's first take a look at *why* He desires purity in our lives. As Christians, we need to have purity with a purpose—and that purpose is love, not piety or self-righteousness. First Peter 1:22-23 offers insight into this: "Now that you have purified yourselves by obeying the truth so that you have sincere love for your brothers, love one another deeply, from the heart. For you have been born again, not of perishable seed, but of imperishable, through the living and enduring word of God." Purity comes by obeying the truth, and this is done so that we have sincere and deep love for our brothers.

When it comes to the areas of our lives where God desires purity, the most obvious one is sexual purity. But we will cover that topic last. First, let's look at some other areas that are also important.

God wants us to have *relational* purity. This means that we esteem and hold our relationships with God, family, and friends in ways that are pure and genuine—free from deceit, selfishness, and being two-faced.

Academic purity is also important. This includes being thorough in our research, careful in our details, and not cheating. *Bodily* purity is another key area. The Bible states that our bodies are living temples of the Holy Spirit and that we should honor God with our bodies because they were purchased by Christ for a great price (1 Corinthians 6:19). *Athletic* purity can include training and eating in honorable ways, competing fairly, and giving glory to God for both our wins and our losses. *Entertainment* purity means simply putting no vile thing before our eyes: "I will be careful to lead a blameless life—when will you come to me? I will walk in my house with blameless heart. I will set before my eyes no vile thing" (Psalm 101:2-3). Purity at *work* means giving it our best and maintaining honor and integrity in our daily transactions.

Sexual purity seems to be one of the key areas where purity is important—especially because it seems to be one of the top areas in which young men struggle. The book of Proverbs has been used for centuries for training the young leaders of Israel (particularly young men during the time of Christ and earlier). Of the 915 verses spanning thirty-one chapters, sexual purity is covered more thoroughly than any other topic pertaining to destructive sins. Gluttony receives some treatment; so does lying and drinking. But sexual sin is a main theme that runs throughout the entire book.

Sexual purity is even put at the top of the list in Scripture passages that encourage purity in various areas of our lives:

> But among you there must not be even a hint of sexual immorality, or of any kind of impurity, or of greed, because these are improper for God's holy people. Nor should there be obscenity, foolish talk, or coarse joking, which are out of place, but rather thanksgiving. For of this you can be sure: No immoral, impure, or greedy person—such a man is an idolater—has any inheritance in the kingdom of Christ and of God (Ephesians 5:3-5).

A true knight realizes that one thoughtless move can possibly ruin a lifetime of achievement—just like a single arrow can knock a knight off his horse if he lets his shield down during a battle charge.

This is why we should avoid sexual sin in both our thoughts as well as our actions (sex outside of marriage).

As a historical example of a knight committed to purity, there is perhaps no better example than Joan of Arc, who was probably the most famous female knight who ever lived. While she was renowned for many of her knightly characteristics and virtues, she was perhaps best known for her purity. Here are a few examples:

- When lying down on a battlefield with an arrow shot completely through from her shoulder to her back, her fellow soldiers offered to "charm" her wound (i.e., use sorcery). Her reply was, "I would rather die than do what I know to be sin."[41]
- In several recorded instances, she used the flat side of her sword to strike the backs of prostitutes that followed her (male) knights into camp after battles. In fact, she broke her sword over the back of one prostitute (which she later regretted).
- She retained her sexual purity her entire life.

Finally, what are some of the practical benefits of living a pure life? First, as we strive to live a life based on purity (keeping in mind, of course, that this is a laudable goal but one that will not be fully achieved while living in our sinful bodies), we gain *power through God* and *boldness before man*: "Dear friends, if our hearts do not condemn us, we have confidence before God and receive from him anything we ask, because we obey his commands and do what pleases him" (1 John 3:21-22).

Such a lifestyle can also lead to an effective prayer life. For example, King David said in Psalm 66:18-19: "If I had cherished sin in my heart, the Lord would not have listened; but God has surely listened and heard my voice in prayer" (see also Deuteronomy 1:42-45). We gain access to God's throne room by no virtue of our own but rather only grace. If we want God's ear in our prayer lives, we need to keep a short list of unrenounced sins. Fortunately, there is forgiveness if we ask with a sincere heart: "If we confess our sins, he is faithful and just and will forgive us our sins and purify us from all unrighteousness" (1 John 1:9).

REFLECT

> She entirely abstained from swearing. I felt myself inspired by her words, for I saw she was in deed a messenger of God; never did I see in her any evil, but always she was as good as if she had been a saint.
>
> —Bertrand De Poulengey, a squire who accompanied Joan of Arc into battle[42]

> Who may ascend the hill of the Lord? Who may stand in his holy place? He who has clean hands and a pure heart, who does not lift up his soul to an idol or swear by what is false. He will receive blessing from the Lord and vindication from God his Savior.
>
> —Psalm 24:3-5

> Do not conform any longer to the pattern of this world, but be transformed by the renewing of your mind. Then you will be able to test and approve what God's will is—his good, pleasing, and perfect will.
>
> —Romans 12:2

> Create in me a pure heart, O God, and renew a steadfast spirit within me.
>
> —Psalm 51:10

Blessed are the pure in heart, for they will see God.

—Matthew 5:8

Every area of our lives is to be under the Lordship of Jesus Christ. And that means the searchlight of God's Word must penetrate every corner of our lives.

—Billy Graham

RESPOND

1. What is the main area of your life where you struggle with purity?
2. How can you rely on God's Word and Christian fellowship to help you improve in this area?
3. How will God's grace and forgiveness help you with your struggle in this area?
4. What benefits flow into our lives when we strive for purity?
5. How can you help others who also struggle in this area?

VIRTUE 18

GALLANTRY

So do not fear, for I am with you; do not be dismayed, for I am your God. I will strengthen you and help you; I will uphold you with my righteous right hand.

—Isaiah 41:10

For I am the LORD your God, who takes hold of your right hand and says to you, "Do not fear; I will help you."

—Isaiah 41:13

Be of good courage, and let us behave ourselves valiantly for our people, and for the cities of our God: and let the LORD do that which is good in his sight.

—1 Chronicles 19:13

Gallantry is one of those rich words that has two meanings. And it so happens that both meanings are spot-on for the training of true knights. The first meaning of the word is essentially "dashing courage" or "heroic bravery." The second meaning of the word is "noble-minded behavior" or giving "courtly attention to women."[43]

In days of old, knights displayed both sides of gallantry when they rode straight at each other in a jousting match and then right after the match brought a rose to their favorite lady in the audience. How's that for a picture of gallantry? Knocking your opponent off his horse and then offering a rose to a lady, all within the same five minutes?

One of the few historians of the fifteenth century to record the traits of knighthood, Ramon Lull, said this about courage: "A knight who is in battle with his Lord, who for lack of courage flees from battle when he should give aid, because he more redoubts or fears the torment or peril more than his courage uses not the office of knighthood." It is safe to assume that gallantry is one of the fundamental aspects of knighthood.[44]

Gallantry is one of the most difficult lessons for a knight to learn because when he attacks his target in wrath or with pride, he may win or lose. But if he wins, he has lost already because the subtle deadly sin of pride will creep under his skin and forge the way he thinks about his next battle. When he conquers a target in such a way—breaking through his opponent's strike, knocking his opponent off his horse in a jousting match—he will start to build up self-reliance, self-will, and self-pride. Then, in his next match, he will likely approach it in much the same way, only to "get knocked off his high horse" as assured by Proverbs 16:18: "Pride goes before destruction, a haughty spirit before a fall."

Herein lies a challenge for all knights that is perhaps the most difficult to win—going forth in pride and self-will versus going forth with confidence in the Lord but trusting also in the natural skill that God has given him. Then, when he wins, all the glory is in the Lord, both for the instance of that victory, as well as the God-given skill that took him through it.

Without a proper and healthy level of gallantry that is grounded in Christ (and not in himself), a knight's game will be off center. Let's work through a few examples.

GALLANTRY IN USING THE SWORD

I enjoy meeting with a group of young men to practice medieval combat skills (we call them "knight nights"). One of the practices we enjoy is cutting tatami mats with medieval swords. Tatami mats are Japanese mats made of reeds. These are then soaked in water, rolled, and set upright on a stand as a cutting target. Watching people cut is amazing. Most of the time you can tell if a swordsman is going to make a clean cut all the way through the mat or if he is going to slice off just part and leave a section of the mat dangling by a few threads (which just taunts and annoys the swordsman).

How can you tell if a swordsman is going to "go clean" even before he swings? It is all in the wind-up, the focus, and the determination. These things, more than physical strength, will define the result of the cut. Swordsmen who go clean have determined in their minds to go clean even before they swing the sword. The best way to describe this is that the successful swordsman does not even see or focus on the mat; they are cutting *through* the mat. The mat *just happens to be in the way of their swing*—a swing that is kept in perfect form *all the way through the slice*. The blade does not move or fold when it hits the mat. The power of the swing does not change. If these steps are done, the mat stands no chance. However, if the swordsman focuses on the mat and expects the mat to respond or push back when struck by the sword, his blade angle will change, his power will reduce, and the mat will win.

These concepts parallel life in so many ways. Can you see the analogy at work, home, and school? Succeeding in a project occurs by confidently moving through the process with internal will and determination—with gallantry. Do not focus on getting the work finished. This will happen automatically if you commit yourself fully to the process.

GALLANTRY IN SPORTS

I enjoy playing tennis with my good friend, Gary. One time, he crushed me in the first two sets. My shots were going long, serves were not coming in strong, and my game was not marked by will or determination. Then, on the third set, I decided to put my full heart, body, and mind into the game. Rather than hitting shots just to get them over the net, I began hitting *through* the ball, and my game completely changed. I took the set and destroyed my racquet in the process. The tempo and will to win I had in the third set was unlike the first two, and it helped me play to the best of my God-given ability, which resulted in a win.

GALLANTRY IN TOURNAMENT COMPETITION

Consider an example from knightly tournaments that involved jousting. Put simply, the knight who won a jousting match was the one who refused to veer away from their opponent at the last second. The lances held by each knight in a jousting tournament were exactly the same size. Both knights had shields and wore full plate mail armor. But the knight who leaned back or tried to avert his opponent at the last second was likely the one who ended up on the ground. The knight who won was most likely the one who *engaged* the battle and *leaned into the process*—regardless of whether it meant their demise or their victory.

GALLANTRY IN BATTLE

The Bible is filled with tales of gallantry. We have David versus Goliath (1 Samuel 17), David's three mighty warriors who broke through enemy lines just to bring him back a canteen of water (2 Samuel 23:26), and Gideon who defeated the Midianites even after God reduced his army from tens of thousands to just three hundred.

Many warriors of old espoused the quality of gallantry. One of the reasons the Vikings were so incredibly courageous in battle is because they believed they were invincible until their appointed time to die in battle. So, in each hand-to-hand, weapon-against-weapon situation, they believed it was their opponent's day to die unless their opponent had their "lucky number." They also believed that warriors who died in battle were carried off by fierce goddess warriors known as the Valkyries to Viking heaven, Valhalla, where they would enjoy an eternal feast. These two beliefs—destiny and reward—gave them unprecedented assurance in battle.

Some of this gallantry and determination is represented in the Viking movie *The 13th Warrior* (1999). One of the scenes in the movie shows a Viking warrior who challenged a local villager to a sword duel to demonstrate that the village was not prepared for a forthcoming battle. When one of the other Viking warriors protested the battle to the Viking chieftain, saying, "Stop this fight now! He is going to get killed!" the chieftain simply replied, "That is possible," and then allowed the fight to continue. He did this because the purpose of having the duel (showing the villagers they were not prepared for a battle) was more important than the safety of the individual swordsman in the duel.

Another scene from the movie shows the Viking warriors heading out to track down and fight the opposing tribe that was battling with the tribe they were defending. When mounting up on horses and heading out, one of the (newer) Viking warriors asks one of the seasoned warriors, "Have we anything resembling a plan?" To this the seasoned warrior simply replies, "Ride till we find them, and kill them all." The determination to win the battle and head out of camp was the necessary first act of courage to start the process of winning the war.

I am sure this same attitude has actually preceded many warriors in real battles. True knights believe in *principles over circumstances.* Sure, planning is necessary before taking on a major challenge in life (indeed we are instructed by Proverbs 20:18, "Make plans by seeking advice; if you wage war, obtain guidance"), but it takes courage and gallantry to "saddle up and go find the bad guys."

Even more modern stories exist of gallantry in the midst of battle. Wyatt Earp was arguably one of the most well-known gunfighters/lawmen in history. In the famous Gunfight at the OK Corral, a little-known fact shows just how brave and intentional he was, particularly during the gunfight itself.

While giving sworn testimony about his involvement in the gunfight, Wyatt offered this background regarding three of the gang members who opposed him and two other lawmen during the fight: "I heard of John Ringo shooting a man down in cold blood near Camp Thomas. I was satisfied that Frank and Tom McLaury killed and robbed Mexicans in Skeleton Canyon about three or four months ago, and I naturally kept my eyes open and did not intend that any of the gang should get the drop on me if I could help it."

Wyatt knew who the best gunfighters were. He took that knowledge into the gunfight and acted on it in such a way that demonstrated gallantry beyond levels that many today would in such a fight. Wyatt's testimony explains his involvement in the gunfight against these three opponents:

> I saw that Billy Clanton and Frank and Tom McLaury had their hands by their sides; Frank McLaury and Billy Clanton's six-shooters were in plain sight. Virgil said, "Throw up your hands; I have come to disarm you!" Billy Clanton and Frank McLaury laid their hands on their six-shooters. Virgil said, "Hold, I don't mean that! I have come to disarm you!" Then Billy Clanton and Frank McLaury commenced to draw their pistols. At the same time, Tom McLaury throwed his hand to his right hip, throwing his coat open like this [showing how] and jumped behind his horse.
>
> I had my pistol in my overcoat pocket, where I had put it when Behan told us he had disarmed the other parties. When I saw Billy Clanton and Frank McLaury draw their pistols, I drew my pistol. Billy Clanton leveled his pistol at me, but I did not aim at him. I knew that Frank McLaury had the reputation of being a good shot and a dangerous man, and I aimed at Frank McLaury. The first two shots were

fired by Billy Clanton and myself, he shooting at me, and I shooting at Frank McLaury. I don't know which was fired first. We fired almost together. The fight then became general.[45]

While Wyatt saw Billy Clanton level his pistol directly at him, he directed his aim at Frank McLaury, whom he knew to be a better gunfighter. Sometimes in life we need to do the same—intentionally aim at one threat while another is pointed right at us. Fortunately for Wyatt, Billy missed; Wyatt did not.

Sometimes such gallantry and determination is needed in a knight's life along with inner will. It may not need to be as reckless as these examples, but sometimes it does.

THE SOURCE OF GALLANTRY

As Christians in spiritual battle, we have the same type of assurance the Vikings had in physical battle—destiny and reward—but ours is even better because *it is real*. As Christians, we can be assured through our battles in life because our destiny and reward are sealed: "For to me, to live is Christ and to die is gain" (Philippians 1:21). Living under such a reality gives us strength and courage beyond what the world can give. In short, we can have confidence because, in death or in life, we are the Lord's.

In the movie *First Knight* (1995), Sir Lancelot wins a sword duel by knocking the sword out of his opponent's hand. Both embarrassed and impressed, his opponent asks, "How did you do that? Was that a trick?" "No," replies Lancelot, "It was no trick—that's how I fight." His opponent replies, "Can I do it? Tell me. I can learn." To this, Lancelot says: "You have to study your opponent, how he moves, so you know what he's going to do before he does it." His opponent, now turned into Lancelot's student, confidently says, "I can do that." Lancelot adds, "You have to know that one moment in every fight, whether you win or lose, and you have to know how to wait for it." Feeling that this was yet another lesson he could learn, his opponent replies, "I can do that." Then Lancelot adds a final criteria, "And you have to not care whether you live or die," to which his opponent does not reply. He was not prepared to make that level of full commitment, so he was not likely to achieve the same ability in fighting as his teacher.

Put simply, a knight cannot reach his full potential and calling in life unless he is completely sold out. He will never be brave enough to accomplish his maximum purpose and calling unless he is in *all the way*. This is the only way that knights of old could live up to the command of the Order, which required a knight to "never turn his back upon a foe." The source of true gallantry is full commitment to Christ.

REFLECT

> He holds victory in store for the upright, he is a shield to those whose walk is blameless, for he guards the course of the just and protects the way of his faithful ones.
>
> —Proverbs 2:7-8

> I love you, O Lord, my strength. The Lord is my rock, my fortress, and my deliverer; my God is my rock, in whom I take refuge. He is my shield and the horn of my salvation, my stronghold.
>
> —Psalm 18:1-2

> If we would endeavor like men of courage to stand in the battle, surely we should feel the favorable assistance of God from Heaven. For He who gives us occasion to fight, to the end we may get the victory, is ready to succor those that fight manfully, and do trust in His grace.[46]

—Thomas à Kempis

If you want to find true bravery, look for it where you see faith, hope, charity, justice, strength, loyalty, and other noble virtues. By these qualities the heart of a noble Knight is guarded from wickedness, treachery, and from the enemies of knighthood.[47]

—Ramon Lull

I do not fear their soldiers; my way lies open. If there are soldiers on the road, I have my Lord with me, who will make a road for me to reach the Dauphin. I was born for this.[48]

—Joan of Arc to Henri Le Royer

RESPOND

1. In what area of your life do you need more gallantry?
2. How could life actually be easier if we were more gallant?
3. How will you be more successful in life if you are fully committed?
4. What is the difference between being brave based on your own confidence and being confident through being filled with the Lord's spirit and direction?
5. How can we be certain that our gallantry is not based in our own abilities but based on the Lord instead (see Zechariah 4:6)?

HOSPITALITY

Share with God's people who are in need. Practice hospitality.

—Romans 12:13

Do not forget to entertain strangers, for by so doing some people have entertained angels without knowing it.

—Hebrews 13:2

Offer hospitality to one another without grumbling.

—1 Peter 4:9

Hospitality simply means going out of your way to serve and provide for others (e.g., by hosting meals, etc.). Does this sound easy? Well, it's actually not so easy for one reason: it takes work and planning. I remember a time when our family was visiting another family who had invited us to their city to enjoy a major parade and celebration. They knew we were coming weeks in advance. When we arrived the day of the parade, they took us through the city to catch glimpses of the festivities here and there, but seeing anything clearly was difficult because of the enormous crowds. When it came time to go out for dinner, all of the restaurants were packed. We tried a waiting list for one that took over an hour and we still could not get seated. Practicing better hospitality would have been to call a good restaurant a few weeks before the parade and have all of the reservations set in advance.

So the lack of hospitality just "goes with the flow" and makes no plans in advance. Practicing hospitality means thinking ahead to the needs of your group and taking steps beforehand to set things up accordingly.

While not as seemingly glorious as other knightly traits like strength, honor, and gallantry, hospitality ranks as one of the key traits of knighthood. In medieval times, there were no planes, trains, or automobiles. Travelers who visited your home needed to stay for at least a few days to regain strength and supplies for their journey onward. We need to do the same for others, particularly for those in the family of believers (Galatians 6:10).

In fact, hospitality is such an important knighthood value that there is an entire knightly order named after it: the Knights Hospitaller. The Knights Hospitaller, also known as the Order of Hospitallers, or simply Hospitallers, was a group of men attached to a hospital in Jerusalem that was founded by Blessed Gerard around 1023. Two Orders of Chivalry (knighthood) evolved from this Order: the Order of the Knights of Saint Lazarus and the Order of the Knights of Saint John, later to be known as the Sovereign Military Order of Malta. The Hospitaller knights provided care for poor, sick, or injured pilgrims to the Holy Land. This Order later became a "religious + military" order and was involved in the First Crusade.

In modern times, true knights need to practice hospitality by being both *intentional* and *prepared*. This means being deliberate about who you ask over and when. Sometimes just "hang out" time with the "regulars" should be replaced with time purposefully poured into those who might really need your time, input, and advice.

REFLECT

But I think it is necessary to send back to you Epaphroditus, my brother, fellow worker, and fellow soldier, who is also your messenger, whom you sent to take care of my needs.

—Philippians 2:25

I have received full payment and even more; I am amply supplied, now that I have received from Epaphroditus the gifts you sent. They are a fragrant offering, an acceptable sacrifice, pleasing to God.

—Philippians 4:18

For even the Son of Man did not come to be served, but to serve, and to give his life as a ransom for many.

—Mark 10:45

Do not forget to entertain strangers, for by so doing some people have entertained angels without knowing it.

—Hebrews 13:2

RESPOND

1. What are some areas in your life where you can be more hospitable?
2. How can being more hospitable impact those around you?
3. How can you improve your hospitality by planning more in advance?
4. How can hospitality be practiced even beyond meals and entertaining?
5. How are we blessed by being more hospitable?

COURTESY

We work hard with our own hands. When we are cursed, we bless; when we are persecuted, we endure it; when we are slandered, we answer kindly.

—1 Corinthians 4:12-13

Let us not become weary in doing good, for at the proper time we will reap a harvest if we do not give up. Therefore, as we have opportunity, let us do good to all people, especially to those who belong to the family of believers.

—Galatians 6:9-10

Do not gloat when your enemy falls; when he stumbles, do not let your heart rejoice, or the LORD will see and disapprove and turn his wrath away from him.

—Proverbs 24:17-18

Most definitions of *courtesy* will include simple action terms, such as "displaying polished manners" or "showing respect for others." More elaborate definitions may describe courtesy as "sophisticated conversation and intellectual skill." The original term comes from the twelfth century term *courteis*, which meant "gentle politeness" and "courtly manners."[49] Regardless of which definition makes the most sense to you, courtesy is something you must see in action—it is not a trait like humility that can just be held internally. I remember seeing my wife's grandfather display courtesy in a very clear and profound way.

My wife's grandparents were married for over sixty years. They were wonderful people, and I learned a lot about what it takes to be a solid husband in a marriage that can withstand the test of time. While they were quite well composed most of the time, they each had their moments of outburst, lost patience, and other challenges that any sixty-year relationship endures. On one such occasion (and apparently this was not the first time), Phil did something (as most husbands often do) that led Pearle to lose her temper, so she hit a few tennis balls at him, one after the other. And Phil just stood there and took it. I was impressed. And I learned a lesson, too: A true knight tames himself to be courteous in all situations—to take the high road and overlook small infractions for love's sake.

Let's consider another example. As a young man, I worked for my father in the family business. He owned the building our company occupied, and a few of our office suites were rented out to other businesses. One winter, we were remodeling the building, and the heating system had to be shut down for a few days. Now, during the dead of winter, this made some of the tenants rightfully angry. One early morning, one of the tenants came to our office and read me the riot act. She was cold, her staff was cold, and she thought it was about time that the heating system was fixed. At the top of her voice and with her finger wagging in my face, she exclaimed, "You go tell your daddy to get the heater fixed or we're moving out next week and not paying rent!" As a young man in my twenties, I could think of nothing worse than telling me to "go find my daddy" to fix a problem. Luckily, before I could say anything in response, she stormed out the door.

When my dad came in the office an hour later, I poured out my frustration. "You wouldn't believe how disrespectful she was to me! She told me to 'go find my daddy'! Can you believe it? I would just prefer it if she did move out!"

My dad let me vent for a while, but then he asked me to do the impossible. "Dan, I know that what she said to you was disrespectful, and I can see that it made you very angry, but I'd like you to go see her before you go home today, apologize to her that the heating system has not been working, and tell her that we'll be sure to get it fixed as soon as possible."

"What?" I exclaimed. "Are you out of your mind? She treated me like an eight-year-old—telling me to 'go find my daddy' while stuffing her finger in my face—and you want me to go apologize to *her*? Give me a break!"

He then explained that sometimes in life you can be right but also be dead right. In other words, yes, she offended me, and I did not deserve her condescending speech. But for me to demand an apology from her, a person who had being paying rent for good service that we were not providing, was not a strategically beneficial move. No matter how unpleasant her message was, it was a valid message nonetheless, and one that we needed to act upon to be diligent landlords.

From my dad's vantage point, our company needed their rent money and the tenant was right: as one of our tenants, it was our job to provide them with top-quality service. Allowing her heating system to go for a few days without working (especially in the winter) was unacceptable. We needed to get it fixed—and fast. She never did apologize to me for the way she acted, but that was okay because the experience helped me grow immeasurably.

Proverbs 26:4-5 provides an apparently contradictory set of proverbial pairs (Proverbs that are topically similar or appear close together in the text). Verse 4 says that we should not answer a fool according to his folly, or we will be just like the fool himself. Verse 5, however, says if we do not answer a fool according to his folly, he will be wise in his own eyes. This seems like quite the conundrum—we're told that the wise should answer a fool and also instructed not to answer the fool. Fortunately, there is a reason for this apparent contradiction. Consider the following truths that are brought out only by the combination of both verses:

- No matter what the circumstances involve, the fool must be kept in his place.
- The folly, but not necessarily the fool bringing the folly, must be answered by the wise.
- There is no routine approach for handling a fool.
- Discernment on the part of the wise is needed in all circumstances.
- Entering into dialogue with a fool is both an obligation and a threat for the wise.

Sometimes a fool needs to be put into his place. In some circumstances, even answering a fool is not a wise choice. In still other circumstances, the allegations of a fool need to be rebutted.

Other important aspects of courtesy when it comes to knighthood include being slow to anger, treating women with respect and gentleness (as the modern term *chivalry* would depict), and having a clean mouth.

BEING SLOW TO ANGER

A true knight does not act, work, or fight battles in anger:

> My dear brothers, take note of this: Everyone should be quick to listen, slow to speak, and slow to become angry, for man's anger does not bring about the righteous life that God desires. Therefore, get rid of all moral filth and the evil that is so prevalent and humbly accept the word planted in you, which can save you (James 1:19-21).

> The end of a matter is better than its beginning, and patience is better than pride. Do not be quickly provoked in your spirit, for anger resides in the lap of fools (Ecclesiastes 7:8-9).

A man's wisdom gives him patience; it is to his glory to overlook an offense (Proverbs 19:11).

Through patience a ruler can be persuaded, and a gentle tongue can break a bone (Proverbs 25:15).

If a ruler's anger rises against you, do not leave your post; calmness can lay great errors to rest (Ecclesiastes 10:4).

TREATING WOMEN WITH RESPECT AND GENTLENESS

A true knight treats women with respect and gentleness:

Husbands love your wives and do not be harsh with them (Colossians 3:19).

Husbands, in the same way be considerate as you live with your wives, and treat them with respect as the weaker partner and as heirs with you of the gracious gift of life, so that nothing will hinder your prayers (1 Peter 3:7).

HAVING A CLEAN MOUTH

Finally, a knight keeps his mouth clean:

With the tongue, we praise our Lord and Father, and with it we curse men, who have been made in God's likeness. Out of the same mouth come praise and cursing. My brothers, this should not be. Can both fresh water and salt water flow from the same spring? My brothers, can a fig tree bear olives, or a grapevine bear figs? Neither can a salt spring produce fresh water (James 3:9-12).

Bless those who persecute you; bless and do not curse (Romans 12:14).

Do not let any unwholesome talk come out of your mouths, but only what is helpful for building others up according to their needs, that it may benefit those who listen (Ephesians 4:29).

REFLECT

It belongs to a Knight to speak nobly and courteously, to have fair armor and be well clad, and to maintain a good and honest household. All of these things are necessary to the honor of knighthood.[50]

—Ramon Lull

Courtesy and knighthood belong together, for villainous and foul words are against the rule of the Order. Loyalty, truth, hardiness, generosity, decency, humility, mercy, and other similar virtues are also essential to knighthood.[51]

—Ramon Lull

RESPOND

1. How is it possible to be courteous to those who treat us rudely?
2. When do you find it most difficult to be courteous to others?
3. In situations that grow tense, how many seconds do you have to choose between making a courteous response and one loaded with anger and no tact?

4. In this century, we have many different ways to respond to people on delicate topics—e-mail, texting, phone, or face-to-face. How can how we respond to someone promote courtesy?

5. Do we owe someone a courteous response even when they treat us rudely?

VIRTUE 21

GRATITUDE

> For who makes you different from anyone else? What do you have that you did not receive? And if you did receive it, why do you boast as though you did not?
>
> —1 Corinthians 4:7
>
> I have learned to be content whatever the circumstances. I know what it is to be in need, and I know what it is to have plenty. I have learned the secret of being content in any and every situation, whether well fed or hungry, whether living in plenty or in want. I can do everything through him who gives me strength.
>
> —Philippians 4:11-14

Gratitude simply means contentment and thankfulness. While having gratitude can enhance our life satisfaction and daily sense of being, the opposite of gratitude (e.g., greed or entitlement) can turn us into bitter, angry people and wreck our daily sense of being.

The knightly trait of gratitude includes both *being* grateful in diverse circumstances as well as *expressing* gratitude to God and others. Toward the latter part of the medieval knight era (the fourteenth to sixteenth centuries), many knights acquired wealth and power and developed relationships with royalty. This wealth and friendship with the king's court brought feasting and abundance in many ways. In fact, part of a squire's training as a knight was "learning how to serve his Lord at meals: the order in which dishes should be presented, where they should be placed, how many fingers to use in holding the joint for the Lord to carve, how to cut the trenchers and place them on the table."[52]

So how does a knight move from the table of kings to pottage for breakfast (a stew made from oats), barley bread for dinner, and the company of a horse and peasants on the battlefield? By having gratitude, that's how. Most people who have lived past their forties have either witnessed extreme plenty and extreme poor or have experienced firsthand these circumstances. The two Bible passages above provide the key on how to live in either circumstance: through Christ.

Do you know someone going through a rough patch in life? Someone who needs to hit rock bottom so they finally change their way of living? One of the ways you can tell they are getting close is by evaluating their level of gratitude. If a person has gone through a rough time and then claims they are finally at rock bottom and ready to cooperate with God's plan, check their level of gratitude. If they are still proud, haughty, and ungrateful, chances are they still have a way to go before hitting bottom. But if they are truly humble and grateful, they may be in a better place—a place where God can start rebuilding their life His way.

I remember going through such a rough patch when I was younger. And I am very grateful (and so are my kids, for there is no telling if they would be alive today) that I chose God's way when presented with some challenging time and life choices. We are all faced with critical junctures in our lives where we are faced with choosing our way or God's way. Fortunately, this was a situation where I chose God's way.

I was seventeen and had saved just enough money, eleven hundred dollars, to buy a motorcycle I had been craving for months (a Yamaha Vision 550). I was especially proud of this purchase because it had low miles, and the person I bought it from also gave me his leather riding jacket and a helmet. However, the helmet, as he pointed out, did not go with the motorcycle because it did not match. The motorcycle was gray, and the helmet was silver with a red stripe and had the word *Turbo* on the side.

I had just brought the motorcycle home and decided to take it out for a quick test run—so quick that I neglected to even put on my new helmet. I was about two blocks from my house, going about thirty mph when a teenager raced his car straight out of his court right in front of me. I had no time to react; all I could do was slam on my brakes and hope to slow down before hitting his car broadside. The impact came, and I flew off the motorcycle straight through the passenger window headfirst. Thankfully, the window was rolled down (I am not sure I would be writing this story if it was not!).

I got up, checked for broken bones (only my wrist was injured), exchanged insurance information, and then walked my wrecked motorcycle home. I was home icing my wounds for about an hour when my girlfriend of about six months called on the phone. When I was about halfway into explaining my rough day to her, she broke the conversation with words that no teenage boyfriend wants to hear: "I am breaking up with you." Shocked, I asked why, and her response took the conversation from bad to really bad. She said, "Because my mom doesn't think you're going anywhere in life—no college plans yet, no promising career opportunities, etc."

So, after losing my life savings, my motorcycle, and my girlfriend, I am now starting to lose my self-esteem. Feeling like things could not get any worse, I started trying to pick up any of the pieces that were left. Then the phone rang again. This time it was my dad, who informed me that one of my friends had racked up a fifteen-hundred-dollar phone bill using his calling card I lent her to make just one call to her boyfriend who had recently moved to another country. So now, not only was I completely broke, I owed more than my entire net worth.

All of this happened within a three-hour time period. After receiving this news, I felt like I was incapable of picking up the pieces and had been hit in the stomach by a battering ram. Looking back at this situation now, I believe I lost everything a teenager could lose—his money, girlfriend, transportation, and future money (by having to pay it to a debt not my own). All of this was erased within hours.

I was faced with the challenge of Job: I could either trust God's purpose for allowing challenge into my life and claim the promise in Romans 8:28 ("All things work together for good for those who love God and are called according to his purpose"), or fall for the temptation to just "curse God and die" (Job 2:9).

That night, I walked to the river, tore off my shirt, and stood before the vast, empty, quiet sky. I asked God to take what was left of my life and to start building it again His way and on His foundation. Up to that day, I had been building my own life with my own choices based on my own desires and teenage whims. Although I became a Christian when I was about eleven, I had not yet given control of my life to Christ. But that night, it all changed, and I relinquished control of my life to God. I resolved to start building the rest of my life from that day forward using the principles of Scripture and to give Him the means and permission to rebuild my life on a solid foundation through my obedience to Him.

That night, I chose to be grateful and humble. Rather than proudly taking charge to rebuild my life on my own foundation, I began building my life on the solid foundation of Christ. Just weeks after making this resolution, God blessed me through healing and encouragement. The insurance company gave me a check for well over the amount of my motorcycle, my wrist was healed, my girlfriend had been forgiven, and my life was starting to come back together.

To top it off, God even did something that allowed me to see His hand in these difficult circumstances. My friend Jason came over to help me find a different motorcycle, and I ended up buying a Yamaha Seca 650 that was silver and red and had "Turbo" painted on the side. After driving the motorcycle home, I set the helmet on the table and then noticed that the new motorcycle exactly matched the helmet that came with the previous motorcycle. In fact, the helmet was actually made to match the red-and-silver Seca Turbo. It was one of those "God moments"—a moment where God showed His signature in the tapestry of my life.

For the next few years, I started building my life on God's promises (e.g., Jeremiah 29:11-12). By going to church, feeding myself with His Word, and striving to live a life of obedience and gratitude, I gave God permission to build my life His way.

I was married four years after this incident. Without telling me, the pastor at our wedding read this passage as a testimony to what God had done in my life:

> Therefore everyone who hears these words of mine and puts them into practice is like a wise man who built his house on the rock. The rain came down, the streams rose, and the winds blew and beat against that house; yet it did not fall, because it had its foundation on the rock. But everyone who hears these words of mine and does not put them into practice is like a foolish man who built his house on sand. The rain came down, the streams rose, and the winds blew and beat against that house, and it fell with a great crash (Matthew 7:24-27).

By choosing gratitude that day rather than rebellion, some means to ease the pain, or a rampage to rebuild my life my way by my methods, I allowed God to use a bulldozer to clear off the land of my future life and to start building it *His* way, with *His* methods, in *His* timing, and using *His* tools. Sadly, it was during this same season that I watched many of my friends make different choices—choices to build their houses on their own (sandy) foundation, only to watch them fall down months or years later.

I can honestly say that my life now would not be the same if I had not chosen gratitude that day. Gratitude enabled me to respond to dire circumstances with an attitude of hopeful expectation. Without being grateful for just having the chance to give what was left of my life to God (rather than needing my life plus money plus girlfriend plus transportation before being grateful), I set myself in a position to allow better times to come—times that God would bring about in His way. I can also honestly say that my life today is not to my own credit. God built my life; I just supplied the willing worker (obedience) to build with His plan, His materials, and His timing.

REFLECT

To that place the Knight was accustomed to come each day in order to pray and adore Almighty God, whom he thanked for all the honors He had shown him throughout his life.[53]

—The Hermit Knight in Ramon Lull's *Book of the Order of Chivalry*

Thankfulness is not some sort of magic formula; it is the language of love, which enables you to communicate effectively with Jesus. A thankful mindset does not entail a denial of reality with its plethora of problems. Instead, it rejoices in Jesus your Savior, in the midst of trials and tribulations.[54]

—Sarah Young

RESPOND

1. How does gratitude stop pride from growing in our hearts?
2. How can having gratitude today shape our lives in the future?
3. Why should we be grateful for our challenges?

4. How is it our choice sometimes whether challenges can make us bitter or shape us for the better? How does gratitude play a role?
5. Sometimes it is easy to take things and people for granted. How can gratitude change this?

GRACE AND MERCY

> Get rid of all bitterness, rage and anger, brawling and slander, along with every form of malice. Be kind and compassionate to one another, forgiving each other, just as in Christ God forgave you.
>
> —Ephesians 4:31-32
>
> Bear with each other and forgive whatever grievances you may have against one another. Forgive as the Lord forgave you. And over all these virtues put on love, which binds them all together in perfect unity.
>
> —Colossians 3:13-14

A true knight needs to live his or her life with both grace *and* mercy. What is the difference between them? Put simply, grace is getting what you *do not* deserve (e.g., a blessing or a reward), while mercy is *not* getting what you deserve (e.g., a punishment).

GRACE

God's grace, for example, is not earned. His grace is offered to us through Christ's sacrifice, even though we do not deserve it: "For it is by grace you have been saved, through faith—and this not from yourselves, it is the gift of God—not by works, so that no one can boast" (Ephesians 2:8-9). We extend grace to others when we treat them with reward or acceptance *even though they might not deserve it.*

Through the process of managing and/or owning a few businesses during my professional career, I have forged several relationships with friends and colleagues. As businesses change and develop in various ways, so do people. New interests emerge and different career tracks are sometimes taken by these friends and colleagues.

Sometimes these departures are cordial, mutually beneficial, and done honorably by each person involved. But sometimes they are not-professional and ethical lines are crossed, feelings are hurt, and trust can be broken on both sides of the departure. When these situations happen, sometimes they cannot be resolved by discussions over the facts, which are oftentimes seen from two very different perspectives.

In such situations, grace might be to extend forgiveness for the person's actions and how he or she has wronged you but not to necessarily continue a relationship. You know that grace has had its way in your heart if you can reflect back on the person or situation and no longer have that bitter sting or pain over the situation. Forgiveness and healing (two of grace's good friends) have removed these.

MERCY

Famous French knight Joan of Arc tried to extend mercy to the English who had invaded her country. Before engaging in battle against the invading English, she wrote them three letters that warned them to retreat or that God's judgment would come through Joan and her French army. Her third and final letter warned,

> You, men of England, who have no right in this kingdom of France, the King of Heaven orders and commands you by me, Joan of Arc, that you quit your strong places, and return to your own country;

if you do not I will cause you such an overthrow as
shall be remembered for all time. I write to you for
the third and last time, and shall write to you no
more.[55]

Joan had this letter fastened to an arrow and shot into the English
camp. The leaders of the English forces read it and boastfully yelled
back, "It is news sent to us from the whore of the French!" Joan's
response to this was amazing. She cried—not out of her feelings
being hurt by being called a whore (Joan was a virgin, so this insult
was deliberate) but out of remorse for the lives of the English, for she
believed that God's judgment had come against them.

The next day, Joan awoke to the entire English force still present
and ready for battle. She rose very early, went to confession, sang
Mass before all her followers, and then led the attack against the
English. The battle lasted all day. The fort was taken, and every single
Englishman died.

Joan was wounded in a battle days after this victory by a
crossbow bolt that punched right through her armor just above her
breast. After applying olive oil and lard to her wound, she returned
to the battlefield crying, "Yield thee to the King of Heaven! You
called me a harlot but I have great pity for your soul, and for your
people."[56]

At this moment, Clasdas (a leader of the English forces), fully
armed from head to foot, fell into the moat and drowned. Joan
was "moved to pity at this sight" and began to weep for the soul of
Clasdas and for all the others who, in great number, were drowned
at the same time. On this same day, all the English who were on the
other side of the bridge were taken and killed.[57] Even in the midst
of battle, she had mercy and a heart of pity for those who opposed
what she believed to be God's will.

Biblical examples of mercy abound. One example comes from 1
Samuel 26 where King Saul was chasing David, hoping to kill him.
Growing tired of hiding out in caves, David decides to sneak up on
King Saul when he is sleeping one night and steal Saul's water jug and

spear. The next morning, he woke up Saul by shouting down from a hilltop, "Here is the king's spear. Let one of your young men come over and get it. The Lord rewards every man for his righteousness and faithfulness. The Lord delivered you into my hands today, but I would not lay a hand on the Lord's anointed" (1 Samuel 26:22-23).

REFLECT

> God has given the Knight a heart to be courageous in his behavior, so ought the Knight to have mercy in his heart and incline his courage to the works of mercy and pity. That is to say, he ought to help and provision to them that approach in tears and require the aid and mercy of Knights, and who have placed all their hope in them.[58]

—Ramon Lull

RESPOND

1. How can showing grace in our dealings with others attract them to (or repel them from) the gospel?
2. How does God's mercy toward us encourage us to be graceful toward others?
3. Is there any area of your life where you have not received God's grace?
4. Is there any area of your life where you have not received God's mercy?
5. What can happen in our hearts if we do not extend grace and mercy to others?

VIRTUE 23

MENTORSHIP

And the things you have heard me say in the presence of many witnesses entrust to reliable men who will also be qualified to teach others. Endure hardship with us like a good soldier of Christ Jesus.

—2 Timothy 2:2-3

As iron sharpens iron, so one man sharpens another.

—Proverbs 27:17

Joab said: "If the Arameans are too strong for me, then you are to rescue me; but if the Ammonites are too strong for you, then I will rescue you. Be strong and let us fight bravely for our people and the cities of our God. The LORD will do what is good in his sight."

—1 Chronicles 19:12-13

Being a mentor to someone means providing him or her with wise and influential counseling when he or she is open to receiving it. Unlike parenting, which can be more direct, mentoring is an exchange of ideas and questions (by the mentee) and advice and input (by the mentor).

Without mentorship, the succession of true values and character traits will die out. I attended a presentation on fatherhood put on by

Focus on the Family where the facilitator asked a pointed question that challenged every dad in the room. He asked, "How many of you have a written plan for raising your kids with Christian values?" About five hands went up in a room of over three hundred. He followed by saying "MTV (Music Television) has a written marketing plan to own your child by age fourteen." The lure of "sex, drugs, and rock and roll" were just some of the tools he outlined in MTV's plan to capture the mind and attention of every young teenager by such a young age. It was shocking.

While I do not actually believe that a parent's plan, or a mentor's plan, absolutely needs to be put in writing, I do think that it should be *intentional and consistent*. The book of Deuteronomy guides us on just exactly how this can be done:

> Love the Lord your God with all your heart and with all your soul and with all your strength. These commandments that I give you today are to be upon your hearts. Impress them on your children. Talk about them when you sit at home and when you walk along the road, when you lie down and when you get up. Tie them as symbols on your hands and bind them on your foreheads. Write them on the doorframes of your houses and on your gates (Deuteronomy 6:5-10).

The practice of mentorship needs to be *constant* and *opportunistic*, but also *timely*. Ephesians 5:16 cautions us to "make the most of every opportunity, because the days are evil." One of the most effective Christians I know goes by the name of Pastor Mark. Mark leads a youth ministry at a large church, and I have seen him in action for several years. Mark makes the most of every opportunity and sometimes even pushes the envelope with new acquaintances. His philosophy is simple: He lives every day like it could be his last, and he does not know if and when he will ever see that person again.

So wherever he can, however he can, he evangelizes and mentors others.

Knighthood and the virtues thereof have only been continued through the ages through mentorship. A true knight leaves a legacy and passes on his virtues to others.

REFLECT

A coat is given to a Knight to symbolize the great ordeals that he must suffer in order to honor knighthood. For just as the coat is worn above the other garments of iron, and faces the rain, and receives blows before they reach the hauberk or other armor, so a Knight is chosen to sustain larger burdens than another man. And all the men who serve under him and are in his care ought, whenever necessary, to seek him out for help; and the Knight should defend them to the extent of his power.

—Ramon Lull

A word aptly spoken is like apples of gold in settings of silver. Like an earring of gold or an ornament of fine gold is a wise man's rebuke to a listening ear. Like the coolness of snow at harvest time is a trustworthy messenger to those who send him; he refreshes the spirit of his masters.

—Proverbs 25:11-13

RESPOND

1. How has your life been impacted by mentors?
2. Who has God brought into your life that needs to be mentored?

3. How can mentors have a more significant impact in our lives than friends and family?
4. Sometimes mentoring others requires using different strategies. Sometimes a mentor should be tactfully direct. In other situations, a mentor should be a consultant, waiting to be asked to give advice, or giving softer advice. When should these different roles be used for mentoring others?
5. What are some of the tools of tactfulness that help in effective mentoring?

VIRTUE 24

OVERCOMING FAILURE

Brothers, I do not consider myself yet to have taken hold of it. But one thing I do: Forgetting what is behind and straining toward what is ahead, I press on toward the goal to win the prize for which God has called me heavenward in Christ Jesus.

—Philippians 3:13-14

If we confess our sins, he is faithful and just and will forgive us our sins and purify us from all unrighteousness.

—1 John 1:9

Because of the LORD's great love we are not consumed, for his compassions never fail. They are new every morning; great is your faithfulness.

—Lamentations 3:22-23

Overcoming failure means getting back up after getting knocked down. It means pushing through a difficult and trying circumstance and not giving up.

Most movies about knights show the gallantry *and pride* of knights as they move from one victorious battle to another victorious battle. But that's not the way of a knight—not then and not now. True knights are familiar with both victory *and* defeat. No matter how hard you train, how much you practice, and how much you prepare, there will always be one better. The knights of old knew this, primarily through their experience in tournaments and not necessarily through their experience in battle.

Tournaments involved swordplay and jousting, two sports that could be incredibly hard on the body. Swordplay (even while armored), led to broken and bruised fingers, hands, and wrists. Jousting (where two opponents charged each other on horseback with pointed lances) led to broken bones and broken egos, as it is easy for both of these to break when being knocked clear off the backside of your horse! In fact, jousting led to so many injuries that King Henry II (1154-1189) forbid the sport to preserve the well-being of his highly trained knights.

Back then, it took a lot of self will and faith in God to get up and face the crowd after being knocked off one's horse by an opponent or being beat down by another during a sword duel that was viewed by peers and relatives. But this is precisely how a knight defeats one of his own worst enemies: pride. In fact, experiencing personal defeat is one of the surest and fastest ways to destroy this key opponent. And in this way, we can grow tremendously through our defeats.

Remember—God is more willing to raise up the humble than he is the proud (1 Peter 5:5-6). If we respond to life's failures with humility toward both God and man and allow our lowly spirit to be corrected, God raises us back to stability and security: "And the God of all grace, who called you to his eternal glory in Christ, after you have suffered a little while, will himself restore you and make you strong, firm, and steadfast" (1 Peter 5:10).

Without properly handling defeat, there is no real success. Success by the nature of our failures embodies a determined spirit to overcome defeat and failure. But we cannot do this on our own. We need God's grace both in discovering our subtle sins and in making appropriate changes.

REFLECT

Therefore we do not lose heart. Though outwardly we are wasting away, yet inwardly we are being renewed day by day. For our light and momentary troubles are achieving for us an eternal glory that far outweighs them all. So we fix our eyes not on what is seen, but on what is unseen. For what is seen is temporary, but what is unseen is eternal.

—2 Corinthians 4:16-18

Endure hardship as discipline; God is treating you as sons. For what son is not disciplined by his father?

—Hebrews 12:7

RESPOND

1. What is the most challenging failure you have experienced? How did you overcome?
2. How does our view of eternity impact how we go through daily challenges?
3. How can God use our failures to build our lives?
4. Sometimes we decide how we will handle our failures even seconds after making them. How can we choose wisely?
5. How does our perspective of the failure impact how we respond to the failure (see Hebrews 12:7)?

THE SEVEN DEADLY SINS

Now that we have covered the twenty-four virtues that hold up a knight's life like pillars, we need to cover what can destroy the life of a knight.

If you were an aspiring knight in the Middle Ages, chances are you would have been trained to avoid the Seven Deadly Sins: Pride, Envy, Gluttony, Greed, Anger, Lust, and Sloth.[59] These seven major or key sins have several references in medieval texts, but perhaps one of the most well-known is included in the book *The Summa de Vitiis* (or "Sum of the Vices") by the French Dominican William Peraldus, written in 1236. According to Michael Evans,[60] Peraldus' work was the "most ambitious of the scholastic treatises on the vices (deadly sins); it was also among the most widely circulated, the most influential, and the most original." Perhaps one of the reasons that Peraldus' work was so prominent during the Middle Ages was because of the painting included that framed the Seven Deadly Sins as grotesque enemies of the soul of the Christian knight. This image is provided on the following pages.

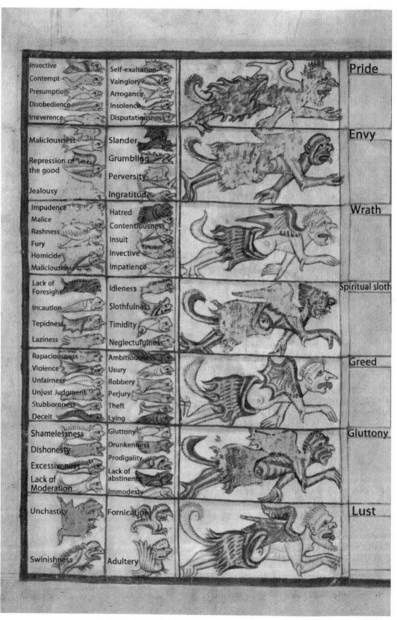

			Pride
Invective	Self-exaltation		
Contempt	Vainglory		
Presumption	Arrogance		
Disobedience	Insolence		
Irreverence	Disputatiousness		
			Envy
Maliciousness	Slander		
Repression of the good	Grumbling		
	Perversity		
Jealousy	Ingratitude		
Impudence	Hatred		Wrath
Malice	Contentiousness		
Rashness	Insult		
Fury	Invective		
Homicide			
Maliciousness	Impatience		
Lack of Foresight	Idleness		Spiritual sloth
Incaution	Slothfulness		
Tepidness	Timidity		
Laziness	Neglectfulness		
Rapaciousness	Ambitiousness		Greed
Violence	Usury		
Unfairness	Robbery		
Unjust Judgment	Perjury		
Stubbornness	Theft		
Deceit	Lying		
Shamelessness	Gluttony		Gluttony
Dishonesty	Drunkenness		
Excessiveness	Prodigality		
Lack of Moderation	Lack of abstinence		
	Immodesty		
Unchastity	Fornication		Lust
Swinishness	Adultery		

"Illumination from William of Peraldus, *Summa de Vitiis*." British Library

154

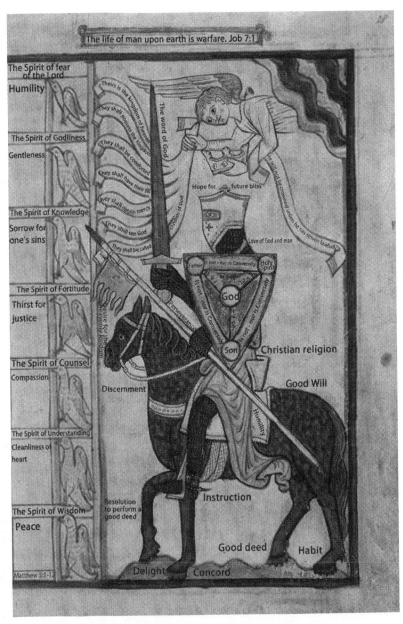

The life of man upon earth is warfare. Job 7:1

The Spirit of fear of the Lord
Humility

The Spirit of Godliness
Gentleness

The Spirit of Knowledge
Sorrow for one's sins

The Spirit of Fortitude
Thirst for justice

The Spirit of Counsel
Compassion

The Spirit of Understanding
Cleanliness of heart

The Spirit of Wisdom
Peace

Matthew 5:1-12

Theirs is the kingdom of heaven
They shall possess the land
They shall be comforted
They shall have their fill
They shall obtain mercy
They shall see God
They shall be called

The word of God

Hope for future bliss

Love of God and man

Father • is not • Nor is • Conversely • Holy Spirit
God
Son
Is not • nor is • Conversely
Desire for the heavenly kingdom
Perseverance

Discernment

Christian religion

Good Will

Humility

Resolution to perform a good deed

Instruction

Delight   Concord

Good deed   Habit

Harley Manuscript 3244. © British Library Board. Used with permission.

155

Daniel A. Biddle

Provided only in ancient Latin, the meaning and symbolism represented in this painting were essentially kept hidden from most readers for centuries. In fact, after hours of research, only partial interpretations of this image could be found on this specific work. After recruiting a couple of ancient Latin experts, each word on the painting has now been translated into modern-day English for the first time.[61]

The heading at the top of the painting states, "The life of man upon earth is warfare" (Job 7:1). Even modern-day knights like the Reverend Billy Graham believed this reality: "I am engaged in spiritual warfare every day. I must never let down my guard."[62] This header sets the stage for the spiritual warfare that is depicted in the image, with the entire right-hand side of the image representing the knight with his vast array of spiritual power (given by God), armor, and weaponry. The entire left-hand side shows his foe, which includes the Seven Deadly Sins followed by sixty-nine horrific monsters representing aspects of each.

On the right-hand side of the image, a knight is shown dressed in thirteenth century armor and weapons that are labeled with Christian qualities and virtues. The knight is being crowned by an angel of the Lord who carries a banner in his left hand that states, "He [the knight] will not be crowned unless he has striven lawfully" (2 Timothy 2:5). The trumpet in the angel's right hand has seven horns that set out the Beatitudes from Matthew 5:3-10. Interestingly, the preface from each of the Beatitudes is removed, and only the "promise" aspect of each is provided.

The angel is preceded by seven doves representing the Seven Gifts of the Holy Spirit:[63] Fear of the Lord, Godliness, Knowledge, Fortitude (strength), Counsel, Understanding, and Wisdom. Immediately below each of these (and directly opposite each of the Seven Deadly Sins) are the first sections of each of the Beatitudes (e.g., Matthew 5:3, "Blessed are the poor in spirit [poverty], theirs is the kingdom of heaven" [shown in the topmost horn in the angel's trumpet]). The English translation of each word on the Peraldus painting is provided in the following table.

English Translation of the Latin Peraldus Image
The life of man upon earth is warfare (Job 7:1).

		[Images of demons]		The Spirit of	
Invective Contempt Presumption Disobedience Irreverence	Self-exaltation Vainglory Arrogance Insolence Disputatiousness		Pride	The Spirit of Fear of the Lord Poverty	[Angel's banner on left arm:] He will not be crowned unless he has striven lawfully. [Angel's banners in right hand:] [from the Beatitudes]
Maliciousness Repression of the good Jealousy	Slander Grumbling Perversity Ingratitude		Envy	The Spirit of Godliness Gentleness	theirs is the kingdom of heaven they shall possess the kingdom
Impudence Malice Rashness Fury Homicide Maliciousness	Hatred Discord Contentiousness Insult Invective Impatience		Wrath	The Spirit of Knowledge Sorrow for [one's] Sins	they shall be comforted they shall have their fill they shall obtain mercy they shall see God
Lack of foresight Incaution Tepidness Laziness	Idleness Slothfulness Timidity Neglectfulness		Spiritual Sloth	The Spirit of Fortitude Thirst for Justice	they shall be called children of God [Shield:] [Upper left corner:] **Father** [Upper right corner:] **[Holy] Spirit**
Rapaciousness Violence Unfairness Unjust judgment Stubbornness Deceit	Ambitiousness Usury Robbery Perjury Theft Lying		Avarice	The Spirit of Counsel Compassion	[Bottom corner:] **Son** [Center:] **God** [Between all three corners:] **Is not—nor [is]** conversely [Items connected with the knight:]
Shamelessness Dishonesty Excessiveness Lack of moderation	Gluttony Drunkenness Prodigality Lack of abstinence Immodesty		Gluttony	The Spirit of Understanding Cleanliness of Heart	[Sword:] **The Word of God** [Helmet:] **Hope for future bliss** [Chain mail:] **Love [of God and fellow human beings]**

Unchastity Swinishness	Fornication Adultery		Lust	The Spirit of Wisdom	[Spear:] **Perseverance** [Banner on spear:]
				Peace	**Desire for the heavenly kingdom** [Reins:] **Discernment** [Saddle:] **Christian religion** [Horse:] **Good will** [Saddle cloth:] **Humility** [Spurs:] **Instruction** [Stirrup:] **Resolution [to perform a] good deed** [Front right hoof:] **Delight** [Front left hoof:] **Concord** [Back right hoof:] **Good deed** [Back left hoof:] **Habit**

While there are no Bible passages that contain the entire list of the seven deadly sins, two come close by including references to most of the seven:

> The acts of the sinful nature are obvious: sexual immorality, impurity and debauchery; idolatry and witchcraft; hatred, discord, jealousy, fits of rage, selfish ambition, dissensions, factions and envy; drunkenness, orgies, and the like. I warn you, as I did before, that those who live like this will not inherit the kingdom of God (Galatians 5:19-21).

> Do you not know that the wicked will not inherit the kingdom of God? Do not be deceived: Neither the sexually immoral nor idolaters nor adulterers nor male prostitutes nor homosexual offenders nor thieves nor the greedy nor drunkards nor slanderers nor swindlers will inherit the kingdom of God. And that is what some of you were. But you were washed, you were sanctified, you were justified in the name

of the Lord Jesus Christ and by the Spirit of our
God (1 Corinthians 6:9-11).

Now let's take a closer look at each of the seven.

PRIDE

Pride is excessive belief in one's own abilities. Pride is said to be the
subtlest of the seven sins—one that grows and matures without the
owner even realizing it. It is also one of the main sins from which
the other sins arise.

Consider this: Proud people act and live *the way they want*. A
line in a popular song says, "I did it my way." If you are doing it
your way and not God's way, you are more likely to get tied up in
the other deadly sins. Humble Christians live God's way because
God said so, not because they necessarily understand why. Proud
Christians rationalize God's Word and commands to conform to
their own lifestyle choices.

A definitive work on the seven deadly sins explains true humility
this way: "The humble person never engages in behavior in order to
achieve honor or glory, but is motivated by benevolence or the glory of
God. When praise is given him he reacts with indifference and thanks
God for having made him an instrument for the benefit of others."[64]

Some key verses on pride:

> For everything in the world—the cravings of sinful
> man, the lust of his eyes, and the boasting of what
> he has and does—comes not from the Father but
> from the world. The world and its desires pass away,
> but the man who does the will of God lives forever
> (1 John 2:16-17).

> When pride comes, then comes disgrace, but with
> humility comes wisdom (Proverbs 11:2).

The fear of the Lord teaches a man wisdom, and humility comes before honor (Proverbs 15:33).

Pride goes before destruction, a haughty spirit before a fall (Proverbs 16:18).

Before his downfall, a man's heart is proud, but humility comes before honor (Proverbs 18:12).

ENVY

Envy is the desire for what others have, including their abilities, gifts, talents, possessions, or situations. Covetousness is part of envy, which is the strong desire for what someone else *possesses*. Jealousy is also part of envy, which is feelings of insecurity, fear, and anxiety over an anticipated loss of something or someone, particularly in reference to a human connection.

Why is envy deadly? Envy like pride is a "stealth invader" in the life of a knight. Envy has a way of sneaking into our thoughts—both conscious and unconscious—to destroy our lives and our effectiveness as Christians.

Envy comes in and begins gnawing at your thoughts: *How can they have this when I only have that? I've worked as hard as they have, but they are paid more.* Or, if you are employed by someone who possesses wealth, *They only have this or that because I've worked to make them rich.* Or for children, *My parents favor my brother (or sister),* or *They've given my sister more opportunities and resources than me.* I have been both the envier and envied of each of these situations. I have seen these thoughts take root in people, alter and change their thoughts, and grip their hearts with such strength that they have become consumed with rage and anger. In fact, you will notice that sometimes the deadly sins will work together—as in the case of anger and envy—to destroy a person's life.

Envious thoughts will come to us all, but those who *stew* in such thoughts will eventually have their hearts and later their actions taken over by envy and all of its related evils (in fact, Proverbs 14:30 even says that "envy rots the bones"). Envy will drive you to be contentious with colleagues, neighbors, and friends, and sometimes *you will not even know that it is envy driving such behaviors*. Envy will drive you to minimize the accomplishments of others (particular those we envy), seek to find fault in them, and call out their weaknesses.

The good news is that there are antidotes to envy. Envy can be removed from your heart through prayer and gratitude. Counting our blessings, both in thought and by our actions, is one effective way for battling envy. Another way is to think through the other person's life from a truly objective standpoint. This is how you can beat envy from a very practical standpoint—by actually retraining how you *think* and what you know about certain people or events.

Consider Jerry Rice, for example. Jerry played 238 games as a wide receiver for the San Francisco 49ers football team. During the season, his performance led him to be recognized by many as the greatest receiver in the history of football. He was the envy of many aspiring football players of that time.

Many probably envied Jerry's abilities without even considering the investment that Jerry made to acquire the skills he developed. First, there was his off-season training routine, which lasted all day. In the morning, he would do cardiovascular work. In the afternoon, he would be in the weight room. In the morning, Jerry would run up a steep five-mile trail. During this run, he would pause at the steepest section and repeat ten, forty-meter wind sprints. Some of Jerry's teammates who tried this conditioning with him were not able to keep up with him. In fact, Roger Craig (another famous 49er) tried running the hill with Rice and said afterward, "I felt like I was going to die." In the afternoon, Jerry's workout in the gym involved 630 repetitions of weight work.

I bet Jerry could tell story after story about how his friends, teammates, and opponents envied his life and his achievements. But how many of those people do you think ever bothered to look into what made Jerry such a great player? Even better, how many others do you think tried to match Jerry's training routine? While many others were enjoying off-season rest and stardom, Jerry was running hills.

In the white-collar work world, similar situations emerge. Others frequently envy the lifestyle and income of executives and professionals as a result of years of diligent work and discipline. The wealth amassed by senior financial investors is often envied by young aspiring professionals—many of whom do not stop to consider the early morning research done six days a week for three decades that has helped lead to their success.

During my training season in life, I was both a full-time student and a full-time employee for seven years. Most of my weekend and evenings were spent in either of these areas with whatever free time I had invested in the family. This discipline was a necessary investment for my calling in life. While others have envied me, seldom have they asked me about the training and investment season that preceded the later seasons of my life.

Some key verses on envy:

> Resentment kills a fool, and envy slays the simple (Job 5:2).

> Do not envy a violent man or choose any of his ways, for the Lord detests a perverse man but takes the upright into his confidence (Proverbs 3:31-32).

> A heart at peace gives life to the body, but envy rots the bones (Proverbs 14:30).

> Do not fret because of evil men or be envious of those who do wrong; for like the grass they will soon wither, like green plants they will soon die away (Psalm 37:1-2).

Finally, consider that envy, or covetousness, is one of the Ten Commandments: "You shall not covet your neighbor's house.

You shall not covet your neighbor's wife, or his manservant or maidservant, his ox or donkey, or anything that belongs to your neighbor" (Exodus 20:17).

A final thought about envy. Humility can be a very effective way to shield your heart against envy. We are admonished in Philippians 2:3 to "do nothing out of selfish ambition or vain conceit, but in humility *consider others better than yourselves*" (emphasis added). If we apply this verse in a very practical way, we can be shielded against the deadly sin of envy.

GLUTTONY

Gluttony is an over-the-top desire to consume or own more than we need. This sin typically refers to food and eating, but it can also be applied to things we own (or want to own) that are beyond our needs. This is not to say that our desire for things we do not need is necessarily sinful, but it can be if we gloat or obsess about amassing more and more things well beyond our short-term and long-term needs.

Here is a simple example of gluttony that does not involve food. I consider myself a flashlight-o-holic; I simply have a hard time entering a hardware store without buying a flashlight. There is something inside of me that loves the newest, brightest technology. Besides, I just know there's going to be that one time on some dark road when my car breaks down and I am going to need a super-bright flashlight with six hours of runtime that uses only two AA batteries. I now try to give away my extras, and I have stopped buying so many (well, I am working on it).

Some key verses on gluttony:

> After fasting forty days and forty nights, he was hungry. The tempter came to him and said, "If you are the Son of God, tell these stones to become bread." Jesus answered, "It is written: 'Man does not

163

live on bread alone, but on every word that comes from the mouth of God'" (Matthew 4:2-4).

Do not join those who drink too much wine or gorge themselves on meat, for drunkards and gluttons become poor, and drowsiness clothes them in rags (Proverbs 23:20-21).

It is interesting that the Bible frequently equates gluttony with the "godless," showing that those who do not have their heart set on something higher (God's interests) are more prone to be obsessed with the fundamental desires of the flesh:

I urge you, brothers, to watch out for those who cause divisions and put obstacles in your way that are contrary to the teaching you have learned. Keep away from them. For such people are not serving our Lord Christ, but their own appetites. By smooth talk and flattery they deceive the minds of naive people" (Romans 16:17-18).

For, as I have often told you before and now say again even with tears, many live as enemies of the cross of Christ. Their destiny is destruction, their god is their stomach, and their glory is in their shame. Their mind is on earthly things (Philippians 3:18-19).

GREED

Greed is the desire for material wealth or gain, ignoring the realm of the spiritual. It is also called avarice in some of the earlier writings on knighthood. Before unpacking this deadly sin, let's first dispel some myths about riches and wealth.

First, acquiring and growing financial resources *and giving*, should this be one of your spiritual and natural gifts, is a good thing.

Romans 12:6-8 explains that God has bestowed several different, but equally important, spiritual gifts to the body of Christ. And giving is right up there with teaching, encouraging, and serving:

> We have different gifts, according to the grace given us. If a man's gift is prophesying, let him use it in proportion to his faith. If it is serving, let him serve; if it is teaching, let him teach; if it is encouraging, let him encourage; if it is contributing to the needs of others, let him give generously; if it is leadership, let him govern diligently; if it is showing mercy, let him do it cheerfully.

Jesus Himself equates responsibility with worldly wealth as a prerequisite for being able to handle spiritual wealth: "Whoever can be trusted with very little can also be trusted with much, and whoever is dishonest with very little will also be dishonest with much. So if you have not been trustworthy in handling worldly wealth, who will trust you with true riches?" (Luke 16:10-11).

A true knight acknowledges that wealth is nothing more than a resource for doing good, first for his family and then for his extended family and the family of God. As long as his heart is set this way, there is nothing wrong with accumulating more and more wealth, provided that he *flows it into action when the Lord calls for it.*

Joseph stored up resources under his stewardship that were later used to feed his father Jacob and his whole family (seventy-five in all) (see Genesis 41 and Acts 7). God used a believer named Agabus to predict that a severe famine would spread over the entire Roman world and then used the disciples, each according to his ability, to provide financial aid to Christians living in Judea (see Acts 11:28-30).

So much of what has to be said about wealth and greed honestly depends on a person's standing with God (their maturity level) as well as their calling in life. If you are married, your spouse should also be in agreement with *both* your wealth building and distribution strategies.

Possessing wealth and taking actions like those described above describe the positive aspects of wealth and how wealth can be used for good. However, there is, of course, a flipside. This is where wealth and the desire for *more* wealth can turn into a deadly sin. Consider these key verses on greed:

> Then he said to them, "Watch out! Be on your guard against all kinds of greed; a man's life does not consist in the abundance of his possessions" (Luke 12:15).

> Do not trust in extortion or take pride in stolen goods; though your riches increase, do not set your heart on them (Psalm 62:10).

> But if we have food and clothing, we will be content with that. People who want to get rich fall into temptation and a trap and into many foolish and harmful desires that plunge men into ruin and destruction. For the love of money is a root of all kinds of evil. Some people, eager for money, have wandered from the faith and pierced themselves with many griefs (1 Timothy 6:8-10).

We are instructed in Scripture to *be on guard* against greed, *not have our hearts set upon riches*, and to *practice contentment* to avoid the pitfalls caused by greed.

ANGER

Anger is a God-given emotion. Scripture even records two instances where Jesus Himself got angry:

He looked around at them in anger and, deeply distressed at their stubborn hearts, said to the man, "Stretch out your hand." He stretched it out, and his hand was completely restored. Then the Pharisees went out and began to plot with the Herodians how they might kill Jesus (Mark 3:5).

Jesus entered the temple area and drove out all who were buying and selling there. He overturned the tables of the moneychangers and the benches of those selling doves. "It is written," he said to them," 'My house will be called a house of prayer,' but you are making it a 'den of robbers.'" (Matthew 21:12-13).

While anger is a God-given emotion, it is typically not handled by most of us in a godly way as Jesus did in the two examples above. Although He was angry and expressed his anger, He did so without sinning).

In the context of deadly sins, anger (or wrath) is not necessarily referring to the occasional outburst that many of us may have experienced. Anger does not typically turn into a deadly sin when it is quickly passed through one's system. In fact, that's just what Scripture encourages us to do with anger—allow it to quickly pass through our system but without sinning. Consider these key verses on anger:

> In your anger do not sin: Do not let the sun go down while you are still angry, and do not give the devil a foothold" (Ephesians 4:26-27). The King James Version puts it this way: "*Be ye angry*, and sin not: let not the sun go down upon your wrath" (emphasis added). Notice that being angry is not the sin; in fact, being angry in the form of experiencing our anger is encouraged.

> Get rid of all bitterness, rage and anger, brawling and slander, along with every form of malice. Be kind and compassionate to one another, forgiving each

other, just as in Christ God forgave you (Ephesians 5:31-32).

But now you must rid yourselves of all such things as these: anger, rage, malice, slander, and filthy language from your lips (Colossians 3:8).

My dear brothers, take note of this: Everyone should be quick to listen, slow to speak, and slow to become angry, for man's anger does not bring about the righteous life that God desires. Therefore, get rid of all moral filth and the evil that is so prevalent and humbly accept the word planted in you, which can save you (James 1:19-21).

The four passages above meld into a single key message regarding anger: be angry, express it without sinning, and then be done with it! Anger turns into a deadly sin whenever it is held and cultivated, which enables it to take root into our hearts and take over our thoughts, emotions, and actions.

Lust

Lust is an inordinate craving for the pleasures of the body. While this typically means lusting of a sexual nature, it can include other objects of our attention and affection. I am in my forties right now, and I have yet to meet a man who has not struggled with lust. While many would say that women tend to struggle most with the deadly sins of pride and envy, men clearly struggle intensely with lust.

Jesus closely equated sexual sin of the mind (i.e., fantasizing) with the actual sins of adultery and fornication (sex outside of marriage). Consider the following verses:

But I tell you that anyone who looks at a woman lustfully has already committed adultery with her in his heart (Matthew 5:28).

You shall not covet your neighbor's house. You shall not covet your neighbor's wife, or his manservant or maidservant, his ox or donkey, or anything that belongs to your neighbor (Exodus 20:17).

Martin Luther offers advice for avoiding lustful thoughts. He also explains how we are responsible for (and in control of) what we think about: "You should follow the advice of a hermit who was approached by a young man complaining of having lustful thoughts and other temptations. The old man told him, 'You can't stop the birds from flying over your head, but only let them fly. Do not let them nest in your hair!' "[65]

We will all have lustful thoughts, but we can *choose* whether or not we dwell on them. It is not the introduction of the thought that is sin, but rather the *dwelling* on the thought that is, or the action therefrom.

SLOTH

Sloth is simply the avoidance of physical or spiritual work. It should not be confused with resting, which we all need to do (God has assigned us all a lifestyle of working six days and resting the seventh). The Bible takes idle living very seriously. God is not pleased with those who squander their God-given talents, abilities, and opportunities by being a "sluggard" as referenced in the Proverbs.

Nowadays, many of us say we are resting and recuperating in front of the TV after work or school, but that can constitute slothfulness. For example, Ecclesiastes 11:6 encourages us to make the most of *all* of our time, including both our day job and evening job: "Sow your seed in the morning, and at evening let not your hands be idle, for you do not know which will succeed, whether this or that, or whether both will do equally well." Yes, there is a time and place for rest, including the occasional "vegging out" in front of the TV or a movie. But every night? And for how long? Consider the following admonishments from Proverbs about using our time effectively and what can happen if we do not:

> Go to the ant, you sluggard; consider its ways and be wise! It has no commander, no overseer or ruler, yet it stores its provisions in summer and gathers its food at harvest. How long will you lie there, you sluggard? When will you get up from your sleep? A little sleep, a little slumber, a little folding of the hands to rest—and poverty will come on you like a bandit and scarcity like an armed man (6:6-11).

> Lazy hands make a man poor, but diligent hands bring wealth (10:4).

> The sluggard craves and gets nothing, but the desires of the diligent are fully satisfied (13:4).

> The way of the sluggard is blocked with thorns, but the path of the upright is a highway (15:19).

> The sluggard buries his hand in the dish; he will not even bring it back to his mouth! (19:24).

> A sluggard does not plow in season; so at harvest time he looks but finds nothing (20:4).

> The sluggard's craving will be the death of him, because his hands refuse to work. All day long he craves for more, but the righteous give without sparing (21:25-26).

I went past the field of the sluggard, past the vineyard of the man who lacks judgment; thorns had come up everywhere, the ground was covered with weeds, and the stone wall was in ruins. I applied my heart to what I observed and learned a lesson from what I saw: A little sleep, a little slumber, a little folding of the hands to rest—and poverty will come on you like a bandit and scarcity like an armed man (24:30-34).

The sluggard says, 'There is a lion in the road, a fierce lion roaming the streets!' As a door turns on its hinges, so a sluggard turns on his bed. The sluggard buries his hand in the dish; he is too lazy to bring it back to his mouth. The sluggard is wiser in his own eyes than seven men who answer discreetly (26:13-16).

The apostle Paul is the most famous speaker/writer of Christian theology in all of history. Yet during his prime speaking years, he never demanded a speaker fee or stipend. While he was a traveling speaker, he covered his own expenses by working as a tentmaker:

Surely you remember, brothers, our toil and hardship; we worked night and day in order not to be a burden to anyone while we preached the gospel of God to you (1 Thessalonians 2:9).

For you yourselves know how you ought to follow our example. We were not idle when we were with you, nor did we eat anyone's food without paying for it. On the contrary, we worked night and day, laboring and toiling so that we would not be a burden to any of you. We did this, not because we do not have the right to such help, but in order to make ourselves a model for you to follow. For even when we were with you, we gave you this rule: If a man will not work, he shall not eat (2 Thessalonians 3:7-10).

Working hard is actually the *easy* way of doing work because it takes less effort than being lazy *in the long run.* By "putting your elbows into it" rather than slowly mushing your way through the day's work, you will get your work done much faster and leave more time for rest and recuperation. The Lord knows what your best looks like, and *He wants all of it.*

REFLECT

This is what the Lord says: "Stand at the crossroads and look; ask for the ancient paths, ask where the good way is, and walk in it, and you will find rest for your souls."

—Jeremiah 6:16

She was right that reality can be harsh and that you shut your eyes to it only at your peril because if you do not face up to the enemy in all his dark power, then the enemy will come up from behind some dark day and destroy you while you are facing the other way.

—Frederick Buechner

It is not the temptation you have, but the decision you make about them that counts.

—Billy Graham

God promises no easy life or days without troubles, trials, difficulties, and temptations. He never promises that life will be perfect. He does not call His children to a playground, but to a battleground.

—Billy Graham

Temptation: Recognize it for what it is, and then reject it—immediately and without compromise.

—Billy Graham

RESPOND

1. Rank the seven deadly sins in the order that you think they might affect your life the most.
2. How might some of the sins you ranked lower on your list still be very dangerous?
3. What are the most effective ways to combat against these sins?
4. Take a moment to think about the "spiritual armor" described in Ephesians 6:10-20 that God gives us to fight against these seven sins and the other sins that try to come into our lives. We have the belt of Truth, the helmet of Salvation, the breastplate of Righteousness, the shoes of the Gospel of Peace, the shield of Faith, and the sword of the Spirit. Why do you think God gives us five defensive weapons, and only one offensive weapon?

The Rite of Passage: Earning the Privilege of Knighthood

This book provides a challenge followed by a reward. The challenge is for three godly mentors to meet at least twice with the aspiring knight to counsel him through eight of these twenty-four virtues. This simply means meeting together, memorizing the Scripture passages relevant to each of the virtues (provided in the boxes with each virtue), and having the mentor "sign off" on each of the virtues assigned. The reward includes a sword and a ring, both given during a knighting ceremony.

Each of the three mentors pours into the soul of the aspiring knight and oversees the memorization of the eight verses. Mentors may even prepare and oversee personal goals or acts of service related to the virtues. See the "Challenges" section in the Appendix for a list of possible challenges that can be used. Whatever the process, the mentor's goal is to insure that the virtues are thoroughly instilled into the life and soul of the aspiring knight. The stories and supplemental verses written on each of the virtues in this book are only the starting places for this lifelong process.

THE CEREMONY

After the squire (the aspiring knight) has memorized the twenty-four passages and has met with the three mentors for training, he or she is ready for the knighting ceremony. Knighting ceremonies in the peak of the knighthood era took an entire day and night that included an all-night prayer vigil and concluded with the knight being paraded through the streets on his horse so all could applaud his accomplishment.

Below is an abbreviated ceremony that includes the same key ingredients of the original fourteenth century versions but can be done in just one afternoon or evening session. This ceremony includes three parts: (1) the preparation, (2) the vigil, and (3) the knighting. Each is described below in outline form so each ceremony can be customized, if desired.

THE PREPARATION

The squire should take a long bath and shave and then put on clean white clothes (symbolizing purity) and a red robe (symbolizing the blood that was shed by Christ as well as the knight's own blood that might need to be shed for others). The knight's sword and ring should be staged on an altar. The squire then spends an evening (at least two hours) in prayer, meditating over the Scripture verses in the Appendix.

THE CEREMONY SERVICE

The ceremony service should include a recital and the demonstration of strength. These are described below.

To prepare for the ceremony, the ceremony director should have a table (or type of altar) set up with candles and the swords and rings for the knights (and belts of truth, shields, helmets, and breastplates, if available. Subtract from the script below if the ceremony is completed without any of these).

The ceremony director leads the squires through the recital below. The words in bold are read by the director, and the words in italics are repeated by the squires.

What is the knight's promise?

To serve all but love only One.

And who can make a knight?

Only the Lord Almighty and a man who chooses to live like one.

And how does a knight live?

By twenty-four virtues.

And what are a knight's rewards?

Hardships in this life.
Eternal life in heaven by God's grace.
Honor.

Do you enter into this commitment?

Yes, I do, with all of my heart, strength, body, and mind.

Do you know right now how much this oath will cost you?

No, I do not.

But are you still willing to go through it?

Yes, I am, for what should it cost a man to forfeit his soul but gain the whole world?

And who does a knight battle?

The world, himself, and the Devil.

And how does he fight?

By the Sword of the Spirit, the Bible, the gifts of the Holy Spirit, and living by the twenty-four virtues.

And how does he receive power?

Through prayer, praise, and study.

And how is he equipped for battle?

With the full armor of God so he can stand his ground.

And what does he do when he loses a battle?

He remembers that the battle is the Lord's, and he gets back up on his horse. A knight will fail, but he will not give up. He will never turn his back to a foe.

Now tell of the Belt of Truth.

It is firmly buckled around my waist, and it represents the true Christian faith; God's Word, the Bible; and my own honesty.

Now tell of the Breastplate of Righteousness.

It is the righteousness of God, which comes by Christ's sacrifice and my acceptance of Him.

Now tell of the Shield of Faith.

It is my faith, which I can use to extinguish the lies of the Enemy and have confidence to gain ground in my life in spiritual ways and others.

Now tell of the Helmet of Salvation.

It is my salvation that comes through faith by grace.

Now tell of the Sword of the Spirit.

It is the Bible, which I must master and practice daily, lest it be knocked from my hands in battle.

And what does this squire bring in exchange for knighthood?

I bring my life, and I exchange my life for me for God's life for me.

Now who brings this Ring of Knighthood?

[State name of parents or guardians.]

And tell of the Ring?

It shows there are twenty-four virtues, which I must live by. These are: Godliness, Love, Hope, Strength, Humility, Perseverance, Honor, Prudence, Temperance, Faith, Justice, Charity, Sacrifice, Compassion, Loyalty, Truth, Purity, Gallantry, Hospitality, Courtesy, Gratitude, Grace and Mercy, Mentorship, and Overcoming Failure.

And tell of the Inscription?

It shows I am one in one thousand men, chosen and set aside by Christ for His good works.

Now bring the sword. [The ceremony director holds the sword and prays]:

Grant, we pray, O Lord, our prayers, and see fit to bless with the hand of Your majesty this sword which your servant desires to bear, to the end that he may be a defender of the church, of widows, of orphans, and of all servants of God, against the cruelty of pagans, and that he may be the terror and dread of his other enemies, ensuring for him the performance of equitable prosecution and just defense. Amen.

The sword is handed to the squire, who keeps it in front of him as he kneels.

Now tell of the Sword.

The sword slays and wounds with both edges, and its point also stabs. The sword is the knight's noblest weapon, and he too should serve in three ways. He should defend the church, he should also defend the poor and weak against the powerful influence of the rich. And just as a sword pierces whatever it touches, likewise a knight should pierce all heretics and villains, attacking them mercilessly wherever he may find them. The pommel symbolizes the world, for a knight is obliged to defend his king. The guard symbolizes the cross, on which Our Redeemer died to preserve mankind, and every true knight should do likewise, braving death to preserve his brethren. Should he perish in the attempt, his soul will surely go to heaven.

Now the knight is dubbed by two leaders, with one holding his own sword and the other using the knight's sword.

Conclusion:

> You who long for the knightly order, it is fitting you should lead a new life; devoutly keeping watch in prayer, fleeing from sin, pride, and villainy; defending the church; providing for widows and orphans. Be bold and protect the people, be loyal and valiant, taking nothing from others. Thus should a knight rule himself. He should be humble of heart and always work and follow deeds of knighthood. Be loyal in war and travel greatly; he must fight with honor for his lady love; he must keep honor with all, so that he cannot be held to blame. No cowardice should be found in his doings; above all, he should uphold the weak. Thus should a knight rule himself.[66]— Eustace Deschamps

And always remember, as knighthood gives to a knight all that belongs to him, a knight ought to give all his forces to honor knighthood.

Now, all Hail be to Christ, the First Knight

> You are the most excellent of men and your lips have been anointed with grace, since God has blessed you forever. Gird your sword upon your side, O mighty one; clothe yourself with splendor and majesty. In your majesty, ride forth victoriously in behalf of truth, humility, and righteousness. Let your right hand display awesome deeds. Let your sharp arrows pierce the

hearts of the king's enemies. Let the nations fall beneath your feet. Your throne, O God, will last forever and ever; a scepter of justice will be the scepter of your kingdom (Psalm 45:2-6).

Now the ceremony director has the new knights arise, draw their swords, and face the audience (if any), and states:

In the name of our Lord Jesus Christ, I make thee a knight. Be brave, be hardy, and be loyal. Arise, Sir [names of new knights]:

Demonstration of Strength

Immediately after the ceremony, have the knights put on a demonstration of strength and skill for the audience. (Be careful to arrange these in proportion to the squires' physical gifts and abilities.) This can include cutting several tatami mats, spear throwing, archery, or whatever the knight is capable of doing best.

APPENDIX

CHALLENGES

The following are twenty-four challenges that can be used for mentoring young men or women who have committed to this knighting program. Virtues one, two, eleven, and twenty-four require writing short essays. Virtues three, six, fifteen, seventeen, eighteen, and twenty require interviewing parents, grandparents, or mentors. These can all be done together (i.e., by interviewing the same people). Parents may modify this list of challenges to be more age appropriate. Candidates who complete these challenges are encouraged to coordinate with sponsors for being awarded a knight sword and ring.[67]

1. **Godliness:** Write a short essay about how you can live your life in a godly way without appearing self-righteous, judgmental, or better than others. Remember, godliness requires two actions: fleeing sin and pursuing righteousness.
2. **Faith:** Study Hebrews 11 and write a short essay on how to apply faith in your life.
3. **Hope:** Interview two older Christians about how God has met their hopes in this life and for eternity.
4. **Love:** Find a meaningful way to express unconditional love to a person you have previously overlooked in your life.
5. **Justice:** Find a true story of how one person's role in a situation brought about justice that had a positive result.
6. **Prudence:** Interview two older Christians about situations where prudence made a difference in their lives, in either

good ways when it was followed or bad ways when it was not.

7. **Temperance:** Choose an area of your life where more temperance is needed and abstain in that area for one week. Examples include TV or movie watching, language, food (e.g., sugar, refined foods, etc.).

8. **Strength:** Work with a parent, grandparent, or mentor to better a personal physical record you set in the past. (This can be combined with Perseverance below.)

9. **Humility:** Perform a *significant* act of kindness and tell no one about it.

10. **Perseverance**: Work with a parent, grandparent, or mentor to better a personal physical record you set in the past. (This can be combined with Strength above.)

11. **Honor**: Watch a movie about honor. Examples include *Courageous* (2012), *Facing the Giants* (2007), or *Fireproof* (2009). Then write a brief essay about how honor was demonstrated in the movie.

12. **Charity**: Make an act of charity and keep it a secret.

13. **Sacrifice:** Sacrifice something that is significant to you to a worthy cause and keep it a secret.

14. **Compassion:** Make an act of compassion and tell no one about it. Such an act could include donating your time to a charity, such as a homeless shelter or food bank, or reading to patients in a hospital.

15. **Loyalty**: Interview two parents, grandparents, or mentors about situations in their lives where loyalty, or the lack of loyalty, has either positively or negatively impacted their lives.

16. **Truth:** Reconcile a time where you lied about something by telling the truth about the situation now to a parent or mentor. Make it right with those you impacted by not being truthful.

17. **Purity**: Interview two older Christians about areas of their lives where they have made choices of purity that have made a positive impact in their lives and others.

18. **Gallantry**: Interview two parents, grandparents, or mentors about situations that have required gallantry in their lives.

19. **Hospitality:** Host (or help a parent or mentor host) a dinner for friends or family.

20. **Courtesy:** Find an elderly parent, grandparent, or mentor and interview him or her about "old fashioned" courtesy— what courtesy was like during his or her upbringing.

21. **Gratitude**: Write a letter to a parent, mentor, or grandparent explaining how you are grateful for him or her.

22. **Grace and Mercy:** Find two stories in the Bible that involve grace and mercy and explain each to a friend, parent, or mentor.

23. **Mentorship**: Mentor someone younger than you for one week by coaching the younger person on three or four of the lessons you have learned in this book.

24. **Overcoming Failure:** Ask an older Christian to "be on standby" in your life to help you overcome a failure in the future or one that has occurred recently that you still need to work through. It could be a poor grade on a test, some moral failure, or an area of your life where you know you could have done better. Write a short essay on how to respond to failure in a godly way.

MEDITATION SCRIPTURES FOR THE VIGIL

The squire should spend at least two hours in one place, alone in solemn prayer and meditation, using the four passages below. If this is done as a group, separate the squires and allow no talking. The squires should also abstain from food and drink during this time.

PSALMS 119:33-38

> Teach me, O Lord, to follow your decrees; then I will keep them to the end. Give me understanding, and I will keep your law and obey it with all my heart.

Direct me in the path of your commands, for there I find delight. Turn my heart toward your statutes and not toward selfish gain. Turn my eyes away from worthless things; preserve my life according to your word. Fulfill your promise to your servant, so that you may be feared.

PROVERBS 3

My son, do not forget my teaching, but keep my commands in your heart, for they will prolong your life many years and bring you prosperity. Let love and faithfulness never leave you; bind them around your neck, write them on the tablet of your heart. Then you will win favor and a good name in the sight of God and man. Trust in the Lord with all your heart and lean not on your own understanding; in all your ways acknowledge him, and he will make your paths straight. Do not be wise in your own eyes; fear the Lord and shun evil. This will bring health to your body and nourishment to your bones. Honor the Lord with your wealth, with the firstfruits of all your crops; then your barns will be filled to overflowing, and your vats will brim over with new wine. My son, do not despise the Lord's discipline and do not resent his rebuke, because the Lord disciplines those he loves, as a father the son he delights in. Blessed is the man who finds wisdom, the man who gains understanding, for she is more profitable than silver and yields better returns than gold. She is more precious than rubies; nothing you desire can compare with her. Long life is in her right hand; in her left hand are riches and honor. Her ways are pleasant ways, and all her paths are peace. She is a tree of life to those who embrace her; those who lay hold of her will be blessed. By wisdom the Lord laid the earth's foundations, by understanding he set the heavens in place; by his knowledge the deeps were divided, and the clouds let drop the dew. My son, preserve sound judgment and discernment, do not let them out of your sight; they will be life for you, an ornament to grace your neck. Then you will go on your way in safety, and your foot will not stumble; when you lie down, you will not be afraid; when you lie down, your sleep will be sweet. Have no fear of sudden disaster or of the ruin that overtakes the wicked, for the Lord will be your confidence and will keep your foot from being snared. Do not withhold good from those who deserve it, when it is in your power to act. Do not say to your neighbor, "Come back later; I'll give it tomorrow"—when you now have it with you. Do not plot harm against your neighbor, who lives trustfully near you. Do not accuse a man for no reason—when he has done you no harm. Do not envy a violent man or choose any of his ways, for the Lord detests a perverse man but takes the upright into his confidence. The Lord's curse is on the house of the wicked, but he blesses the home of the righteous. He mocks proud mockers but gives grace to the humble. The wise inherit honor, but fools he holds up to shame.

PSALM 86

Hear, O Lord, and answer me, for I am poor and needy. Guard my life, for I am devoted to you. You are my God; save your servant who trusts in you. Have mercy on me, O Lord, for I call to you all day long. Bring joy to your servant, for to you, O Lord, I lift up my soul. You are forgiving and good, O

Lord, abounding in love to all who call to you. Hear my prayer, O Lord? Listen to my cry for mercy. In the day of my trouble I will call to you, for you will answer me. Among the gods there is none like you, O Lord; no deeds can compare with yours. All the nations you have made will come and worship before you, O Lord; they will bring glory to your name. For you are great and do marvelous deeds; you alone are God. Teach me your way, O Lord, and I will walk in your truth; give me an undivided heart, that I may fear your name. I will praise you, O Lord my God, with all my heart; I will glorify your name forever. For great is your love toward me; you have delivered me from the depths of the grave. The arrogant are attacking me, O God; a band of ruthless men seeks my life—men without regard for you. But you, O Lord, are a compassionate and gracious God, slow to anger, abounding in love and faithfulness. Turn to me and have mercy on me; grant your strength to your servant and save the son of your maidservant. Give me a sign of your goodness, that my enemies may see it and be put to shame, for you, O Lord, have helped me and comforted me.

1 TIMOTHY 6:11-12

But you, man of God, flee from all this, and pursue righteousness, godliness, faith, love, endurance, and gentleness. Fight the good fight of the faith. Take hold of the eternal life to which you were called when you made your good confession in the presence of many witnesses.

PSALM 15

Lord, who may dwell in your sanctuary? Who may live on your holy hill? He whose walk is blameless and who does what is righteous, who speaks the truth from his heart and has no slander on his tongue, who does his neighbor no wrong and casts no slur on his fellowman, who despises a vile man but honors those who fear the Lord, who keeps his oath even when it hurts, who lends his money without usury and does not accept a bribe against the innocent. He who does these things will never be shaken.

1 PETER 1-2

To God's elect, strangers in the world, scattered throughout Pontus, Galatia, Cappadocia, Asia, and Bithynia, who have been chosen according to the foreknowledge of God the Father, through the sanctifying work of the Spirit, for obedience to Jesus Christ and sprinkling by his blood: Grace and peace be yours in abundance.

Praise be to the God and Father of our Lord Jesus Christ! In his great mercy, he has given us new birth into a living hope through the resurrection of Jesus Christ from the dead, and into an inheritance that can never perish, spoil, or fade—kept in heaven for you, who through faith are shielded by God's power until the coming of the salvation that is ready to be revealed in the last time.

In this you greatly rejoice, though now for a little while you may have had to suffer grief in all kinds of trials. These have come so that your faith—of greater worth than gold, which perishes even though refined by fire—may be proved genuine and may result in praise, glory, and honor when Jesus Christ is revealed.

Though you have not seen him, you love him; and even though you do not see him now, you believe in him and are filled with an inexpressible and glorious joy, for you are receiving the goal of your faith, the salvation of your souls.

Concerning this salvation, the prophets, who spoke of the grace that was to come to you, searched intently and with the greatest care, trying to find out the time and circumstances to which the Spirit of Christ in them was pointing when he predicted the sufferings of Christ and the glories that would follow.

It was revealed to them that they were not serving themselves but you, when they spoke of the things that have now been told you by those who have preached the gospel to you by the Holy Spirit sent from heaven. Even angels long to look into these things.

Therefore, prepare your minds for action; be self-controlled; set your hope fully on the grace to be given you when Jesus Christ is revealed. As obedient children, do not conform to the evil desires you had when you lived in ignorance. But just as he who called you is holy, so be holy in all you do; for it is written: "Be holy, because I am holy."

Since you call on a Father who judges each man's work impartially, live your lives as strangers here in reverent fear. For you know that it was not with perishable things such as silver or gold that you were redeemed from the empty way of life handed down to you from your forefathers, but with the precious blood of Christ, a lamb without blemish or defect. He was chosen before the creation of the world, but was revealed in these last times for your sake. Through him you believe in God, who raised him from the dead and glorified him, and so your faith and hope are in God.

Now that you have purified yourselves by obeying the truth so that you have sincere love for your brothers, love one another deeply, from the heart. For you have been born again, not of perishable seed, but of imperishable, through the living and enduring word of God.

For, "All men are like grass, and all their glory is like the flowers of the field; the grass withers and the flowers fall, but the word of the Lord stands forever." And this is the word that was preached to you.

Therefore, rid yourselves of all malice and all deceit, hypocrisy, envy, and slander of every kind. Like newborn babies, crave pure spiritual milk so that by it you may grow up in your salvation, now that you have tasted that the Lord is good.

As you come to him, the living Stone—rejected by men but chosen by God and precious to him—you also, like living stones, are being built into a spiritual house to be a holy priesthood, offering spiritual sacrifices acceptable to God through Jesus Christ. For in Scripture it says: "See, I lay a stone in Zion, a chosen and precious cornerstone, and the one who trusts in him will never be put to shame."

Now to you who believe, this stone is precious. But to those who do not believe, "The stone the builders rejected has become the capstone,'" and, "A stone that causes men to stumble and a rock that makes them fall." They stumble because they disobey the message—which is also what they were destined for.

But you are a chosen people, a royal priesthood, a holy nation, a people belonging to God, that you may declare the praises of him who called you out of darkness into his wonderful light. Once you were not a people, but now you are the people of God; once you had not received mercy, but now you have received mercy. Dear friends, I urge you, as aliens and strangers in the world, to abstain from sinful desires, which war against your soul. Live such good lives among the pagans that, though they accuse you of doing wrong, they may see your good deeds and glorify God on the day he visits us.

Submit yourselves for the Lord's sake to every authority instituted among men: whether to the king, as the supreme authority, or to governors, who are sent by him to punish those who do wrong and to commend those who do right. For it is God's will that by doing good you should silence the ignorant talk of foolish men. Live as free men, but do not use your freedom as a cover-up for evil; live as servants of God.

Show proper respect to everyone: Love the brotherhood of believers, fear God, honor the king. Slaves, submit yourselves to your masters with all respect, not only to those who are good and considerate, but also to those who are harsh. For it is commendable if a man bears up under the pain of unjust suffering because he is conscious of God. But how is it to your credit if you receive a beating for doing wrong and endure it? But if you suffer for doing good and you endure it, this is commendable before God.

To this you were called, because Christ suffered for you, leaving you an example that you should follow in his steps. "He committed no sin, and no deceit was found in his mouth." When they hurled their insults at him, he did not retaliate; when he suffered, he made no threats. Instead, he entrusted himself to him who judges justly.

He himself bore our sins in his body on the tree so that we might die to sins and live for righteousness; by his wounds you have been healed. For you were like sheep going astray, but now you have returned to the Shepherd and Overseer of your souls.

Ephesians 3:14-5:21

For this reason, I kneel before the Father, from whom his whole family in heaven and on earth derives its name. I pray that out of his glorious riches he may strengthen you with power through his Spirit in your inner being, so that Christ may dwell in your hearts through faith. And I pray that you, being rooted and established in love, may have power, together with all the saints, to grasp how wide and long and high and deep is the love of Christ, and to know this love that surpasses knowledge—that you may be filled to the measure of all the fullness of God. Now to him who is able to do immeasurably more than all we ask or imagine, according to his power that is at work within us, to him be glory in the church and in Christ Jesus throughout all generations, for ever and ever! Amen.

As a prisoner for the Lord, then, I urge you to live a life worthy of the calling you have received. Be completely humble and gentle; be patient, bearing with one another in love. Make every effort to keep the unity of the Spirit through the bond of peace. There is one body and one Spirit—just as you were called to one hope when you were called—one Lord, one faith, one baptism; one God and Father of all, who is over all and through all and in all.

But to each one of us grace has been given as Christ apportioned it. This is why it says: "When he ascended on high, he led captives in his train and gave gifts to men." What does "he ascended" mean except that he also descended to the lower, earthly regions? He who descended is the very one who ascended higher than all the heavens, in order to fill the whole universe. It was he who gave some to be apostles, some to be prophets, some to be evangelists, and some to be pastors and teachers, to prepare God's people for works of service, so that the body of Christ may be built up until we all reach unity in the faith and in the knowledge of the Son of God and become mature, attaining to the whole measure of the fullness of Christ. Then we will no longer be infants, tossed back and forth by the waves, and blown here and there by every wind of teaching and by the cunning and craftiness of men in their deceitful scheming. Instead, speaking the truth in love, we will in all things grow up into him who is the Head, that is, Christ. From him the whole body, joined and held together by every supporting ligament, grows and builds itself up in love, as each part does its work.

So I tell you this, and insist on it in the Lord, that you must no longer live as the Gentiles do, in the futility of their thinking. They are darkened in their understanding and separated from the life of God because of the ignorance that is in them due to the hardening of their hearts. Having lost all sensitivity, they have given themselves over to sensuality so as to indulge in every kind of impurity, with a continual lust for more. You, however, did not come to know Christ that way. Surely you heard of him and were taught in him in accordance with the truth that is in Jesus. You were taught, with regard to your former way of life, to put off your old self, which is being corrupted by its deceitful desires; to be made new in the attitude of your minds; and to put on the new self, created to be like God in true righteousness and holiness. Therefore each of you must put off falsehood and speak truthfully to his neighbor, for we are all members of one body. "In your anger do not sin": Do not let the sun go down while you are still angry, and do not give the devil a foothold. He who has been stealing must steal no longer, but must work, doing something useful with his own hands, that he may have something to share with those in need. Do not let any unwholesome talk come out of your mouths, but only what is helpful for building others up according to their needs, that it may benefit those who listen. And do not grieve the Holy Spirit of God, with whom you were sealed for the day of redemption. Get rid of all bitterness, rage and anger, brawling and slander, along with every form of malice. Be kind and compassionate to one another, forgiving each other, just as in Christ God forgave you.

Be imitators of God, therefore, as dearly loved children and live a life of love, just as Christ loved us and gave himself up for us as a fragrant offering and sacrifice to God. But among you there must not be even a hint of sexual immorality, or of any kind of impurity, or of greed, because these are improper for God's holy people. Nor should there be obscenity, foolish talk, or coarse joking, which are out of place, but rather thanksgiving. For of this you can be sure: No immoral, impure, or greedy person—such a man is an idolater—has any inheritance in the kingdom of Christ and of God. Let no one deceive you with empty words, for because of such things God's wrath comes on those who are disobedient. Therefore do not be partners with them. For you were once darkness, but now you are light in the Lord. Live as children of light (for the fruit of the light consists in all goodness, righteousness, and truth) and find out what pleases the Lord. Have nothing to do with the fruitless deeds of darkness, but rather expose them. For it is shameful even to mention what the disobedient do in secret. But everything exposed by the light becomes visible, for it is light that makes everything visible. This is why it is said: "Wake up, O sleeper, rise from the dead, and Christ will shine on you." Be very careful, then, how you live—not as unwise but as wise, making the most of every opportunity, because the days are evil. Therefore do not be foolish, but understand what the Lord's will is. Do not get drunk on wine, which leads to debauchery. Instead, be filled with the Spirit. Speak to one another with psalms, hymns, and spiritual songs. Sing and make music in your heart to the Lord, always giving thanks to God the Father for everything, in the name of our Lord Jesus Christ. Submit to one another out of reverence for Christ.

EPHESIANS 6:10-18 (THE ARMOR OF GOD)

Finally, be strong in the Lord and in his mighty power. Put on the full armor of God so that you can take your stand against the devil's schemes. For our struggle is not against flesh and blood, but against the rulers, against the authorities, against the powers of this dark world, and against the spiritual forces of evil in the heavenly realms. Therefore put on the full armor of God, so that when the day of evil comes, you may be able to stand your ground, and after you have done everything, to stand. Stand firm then, with the belt of truth buckled around your waist, with the breastplate of righteousness in place, and with your feet fitted with the readiness that comes from the gospel of peace. In addition to all this, take up the shield of faith, with which you can extinguish all the flaming arrows of the evil one. Take the helmet of salvation and the sword of the Spirit, which is the word of God. And pray in the Spirit on all occasions with all kinds of prayers and requests. With this in mind, be alert and always keep on praying for all the saints.

MARK 10:29-31

"I tell you the truth," Jesus replied, "no one who has left home or brothers or sisters or mother or father or children or fields for me and the gospel will fail to receive a hundred times as much in this present age (homes, brothers, sisters, mothers, children, and fields—and with them, persecutions) and in the age to come, eternal life. But many who are first will be last, and the last first."

JAMES 1:22-25

Do not merely listen to the word, and so deceive yourselves. Do what it says. Anyone who listens to the word but does not do what it says is like a man who looks at his face in a mirror and, after looking at himself, goes away and immediately forgets what he looks like. But the man who looks intently into the perfect law that gives freedom, and continues to do this, not forgetting what he has heard, but doing it—he will be blessed in what he does.

ROMANS 6:1-23

What shall we say, then? Shall we go on sinning so that grace may increase? By no means! We died to sin; how can we live in it any longer? Or don't you know that all of us who were baptized into Christ Jesus were baptized into his death? We were therefore buried with him through baptism into death in order that, just as Christ was raised from the dead through the glory of the Father, we too may live a new life. If we have been united with him like this in his death, we will certainly also be united with him in his resurrection. For we know that our old self was crucified with him so that the body of sin might be done away with, that we should no longer be slaves to sin—because anyone who has died has been freed from sin. Now if we died with Christ, we believe that we will also live with him.

For we know that since Christ was raised from the dead, he cannot die again; death no longer has mastery over him. The death he died, he died to sin once for all; but the life he lives, he lives to God. In the same way, count yourselves dead to sin but alive to God in Christ Jesus. Therefore do not let sin reign in your mortal body so that you obey its evil desires. Do not offer the parts of your body to sin, as instruments of wickedness, but rather offer yourselves to God, as those who have been brought from death to life; and offer the parts of your body to him as instruments of righteousness. For sin shall not be your master, because you are not under law, but under grace.

What then? Shall we sin because we are not under law but under grace? By no means! Don't you know that when you offer yourselves to someone to obey him as slaves, you are slaves to the one whom you obey—whether you are slaves to sin, which leads to death, or to obedience, which leads to righteousness? But thanks be to God that, though you used to be slaves to sin, you wholeheartedly obeyed the form of teaching to which you were entrusted. You have been set free from sin and have become slaves to righteousness. I put this in human terms because you are weak in your natural selves. Just as you used to offer the parts of your body in slavery to impurity and to ever-increasing wickedness, so now offer them in slavery to righteousness leading to holiness. When you were slaves to sin, you were free from the control of righteousness. What benefit did you reap at that time from the things you are now ashamed of? Those things result in death! But now that you have been set free from sin and have become slaves to God, the benefit you reap leads to holiness, and the result is eternal life. For the wages of sin is death, but the gift of God is eternal life in Christ Jesus our Lord.

ENDNOTES

1   Billy Graham. *Hope for a Troubled Heart* (Nashville, TN: Thomas Nelson, 1991), 50.

2   N. T. Wright, *After You Believe: Why Christian Character Matters* (New York, N.Y.: HarperCollins Publishers, 2010), 7.

3   Wright, *After You Believe,* p. 20.

4   Wright, *After You Believe,* p. 197.

5   Oswald Chambers, *My Utmost for His Highest Selections for the Year/the Golden Book of Oswald Chambers: Selections for the Year* (Grand Rapid: MI: Discovery House Publishing, 1993).

6   Used by permission from the Norton Anthology of English Literature. Some content of Lull's work as translated by this source were updated by the author to make the text more accessible for the modern reader. In addition, the "Order of Chivalry" was replaced with the "Order of Knighthood" every time referenced. Readers are encouraged to view the original translation. Available: *http://wwnorton.com/college/english/nael/middleages/topic_1/lull.htm.* (Accessed December 23, 2011). Additional translations are available: *www.rgle.org.uk/Llull_B_C.htm.* (Accessed December 23, 2011).

7   Marina Warner, *The Afterlife of Joan of Arc: The Image of Female Heroism* (Berkeley and Los Angeles, CA: University of California Press, 2000), 234.

8   Elias Ashmore, *Institution, Laws and Ceremonies of the Most Noble Order of the Garter* (London: Angel, 1672).

9   Os Guinness, *Rising to the Call* (Nashville, TN: West Publishing Group, 2003).

10 An example of the five virtues of knighthood can be seen in the story of Sir Gawain and the Green Knight, where Gawain bears a shield with a

five-pointed star, symbolizing the five virtues: franchise, brotherly love, chastity, courtesy, and pity. The twelve virtues of the Knights Code of Chivalry were also described in the 14th Century by the Duke of Burgandy as: Faith, Charity, Justice, Sagacity, Prudence, Temperance, Resolution, Truth, Liberality, Diligence, Hope, and Valor. For additional sources, see: *Knightly Virtues. Wikipedia: http://en.wikipedia.org/wiki/Knightly_Virtues* (December 23, 2011).

[11] Ramon Lull, Norton Anthology of English Literature.

[12] Bernard of Clairvaux, "In Praise of the New Knighthood," The Works of Bernard of Clairvaux, V. 7 (Kalamazoo, MI: Cistercian Publications, 1977), 127-167.

[13] David Guzik, *David Guzik's Commentary on Zechariah:* www.enduringword. com/commentaries/3804.htm. (December 23, 2011).

[14] Polly Brooks, *Beyond the Myth: The Story of Joan of Arc* (Boston, MA: Houghton-Mifflin, 2001), 61.

[15] Ramon Lull, Norton Anthology of English Literature.

[16] Ramon Lull, Norton Anthology of English Literature.

[17] *Wikipedia: http://en.wikipedia.org/wiki/Hope* (April 21, 2012).

[18] William Trask, *Joan of Arc in Her Own Words* (New York: Books & Company, 1996), 34.

[19] Tim Keller, interviewed by Richard Doster, ByFaithOnline, Our Conversation with Tim Keller, Issue Number 31, May 2011.

[20] *Merriam-Webster Online Dictionary: www.merriam-webster.com/dictionary/ prudence* (April 21, 2012).

[21] *Merriam-Webster Online Dictionary: www.merriam-webster.com/dictionary/ sagacious* (April 21, 2012).

[22] *Merriam-Webster Online Dictionary: www.merriam-webster.com/dictionary/ temperance* (April 21, 2012).

[23] ROIWorld, Teens & Social Networks Study (June, 2010). Available: www. scribd.com/doc/33751159/Teens-Social-Networks-Study-June-2010. (December 25, 2011).

[24] Yahoo (2003). *Born to be Wired.* Available: http://us.i1.yimg.com/us.yimg. com/i/promo/btbw_2003/btbw_execsum.pdf (December 25, 2011).

[25] Ramon Lull, Norton Anthology of English Literature.

26 *Wikipedia: http://en.wikipedia.org/wiki/Ralph_Washington_Sockman* (April 21, 2012).

27 Ramon Lull, Norton Anthology of English Literature.

28 Franklin Graham. *Billy Graham in Quotes* (Nashville, TN: Thomas Nelson, 2011), 250.

29 Ramon Lull, Norton Anthology of English Literature.

30 *Quotes DB*: http://www.quotedb.com/quotes/309 (April 21, 2012).

31 *Chivalry Now*: http://www.chivalrynow.net/articles/steven.htm (April 21, 2012).

32 *Merriam-Webster Online Dictionary: www.merriam-webster.com/dictionary/sacrifice* (April 21, 2012).

33 Ed Rickard, "The Key to Success." Bible Study at the Moorings: www.themoorings.org/life/basics/sacr.html August 5, 2011.

34 Elisabeth Elliott, *Through Gates of Splendor* (Carol Stream, IL: Tyndale House, 1986).

35 Ramon Lull, Norton Anthology of English Literature.

36 A.L. Long, *Memoirs of Robert E. Lee* (Birmingham, AL: Book Sales, 1991).

37 R. Paul Stevens, *Married for Good* (Vancouver, BC: Regent College Publishing, 1997).

38 John Newton. "The Marks of Loyalty," From the Pulpit. *St. Paul's Online: www.stpaulshalifax.org/page63.html.* (August 15, 1999).

39 Ramon Lull, Norton Anthology of English Literature.

40 *Merriam-Webster Online Dictionary: www.merriam-webster.com/dictionary/purity* (April 21, 2012).

41 Trask, *Joan of Arc in Her Own Words*, 37.

42 Vaucouleurs and Joinery to Chinon. *St. Joan Online: www.stjoan-center.com/Trials/null04.html* (December 23, 2011).

43 *Merriam-Webster Online Dictionary: www.merriam-webster.com/dictionary/gallantry* (April 21, 2012).

44 Ramon Lull, Norton Anthology of English Literature.

45 Statement of Wyatt S. Earp in the Preliminary Hearing in the Earp-Holliday Case, Heard before Judge Wells Spicer, November 16, 1881: Alford E. Turner, *The O.K. Corral Inquest* (College Station, TX: Early West Publishing, 1992).

46 Thomas à Kempis. *The Imitation of Christ* (New York: NY: Vintage Press, 1998).

47 Ramon Lull, Norton Anthology of English Literature.

48 Trask, *Joan of Arc in Her Own Words*, 19.

49 *Merriam-Webster Online Dictionary: www.merriam-webster.com/dictionary/courteous* (April 21, 2012).

50 Ramon Lull, Norton Anthology of English Literature.

51 Ramon Lull, Norton Anthology of English Literature.

52 Joseph Gies & Frances Gies. *Life in a Medieval Castle* (New York, NY: Harper & Row Publishers, Inc., 1974).

53 Ramon Lull, Norton Anthology of English Literature.

54 Sarah Young. *Jesus Calling: Enjoying Peace in His Presence* (Nashville, TN: Thomas Nelson Publishers, 2004).

55 Trask, *Joan of Arc in Her Own Words*, 35.

56 Joans Friends, Part 2. *St. Joan Online: www.stjoan-center.com/Trials* (April 21, 2012).

57 Joans Friends, Part 2. *St. Joan Online: www.stjoan-center.com/Trials* (December 23, 2011).

58 Ramon Lull, Norton Anthology of English Literature.

59 Readers are encouraged to read a modern work on the Seven Deadly Sins by Robin R. Meyers (*The Virtue in the Vice: Finding the Seven Lively Virtues in the Seven Deadly Sins* (Deerfield Beach, FL: Health Communications, Inc., 2004).

60 Michael Evans. "An Illustrated Fragment of Peraldus' Summa of Vice: Harleian MS 3244." *Journal of the Warburg and Courtauld Institutes, Vol. 45* (1982): 14-68.

61 Dr. Richard Newhauser, Professor in the Department of English at Arizona State University noted that there are currently no modern editions or translations of Peraldus. However, one is currently being prepared by Dr. Newhauser and several colleagues that will include a critical edition with facing-page translations. This work will be published by Oxford University Press. A partial translation is currently made available by Dr. Newhauser at: *www.public.asu.edu/~rnewhaus/peraldus/*. Personal conversation, March 7, 2011.

62   Franklin Graham. *Billy Graham in Quotes* (Nashville, TN: Thomas Nelson, 2011), 221.

63   A full description of these is outlined by St. Thomas Aquinas in the *Summa Theologica*: *Christian Classics Ethereal Library: www.ccel.org/ccel/aquinas/summa.toc.html*.

64   Solomon Schimmel. *The Seven Deadly Sins: Jewish, Christian, and Classical Reflections on Human Psychology* (New York: Oxford University Press, 1997)

65   James Galvin. *Faith Alone: A Daily Devotional* (Grand Rapids, MI: Zondervan, 2005).

66   *Chivalry Now*: http://www.chivalrynow.net/articles/steven.htm (April 21, 2012).

67   Contact the author for help selecting appropriate swords and rings: dabiddle@msn.com.

61809799R00144

Made in the USA
Middletown, DE
15 January 2018